A LONG WAY

FROM

NO GO

Tjanara Goreng Goreng is a Wakka Wakka Wulli Wulli traditional owner from Central Queensland who was born in Longreach. She has spent a total of 40 years as a public servant and an academic, and was one of the bright young people taken on by Charlie Perkins, the first Indigenous person to head up the Department of Aboriginal Affairs.

In 2006, she was suspended and later, resigned, from her position in the Office of Indigenous Policy Coordination in the Prime Minister's Department after she turned whistleblower and helped expose the Howard government's fraudulent claims leading up to the intervention into Northern Territory Aboriginal communities.

Tjanara is currently an Adjunct Assistant Professor in Indigenous Studies at the University of Canberra while completing her PhD at the Australian National University. She is the founder of The Foundation for Indigenous Recovery and Development Australia, and is also a member of the National Indigenous Research Knowledge's Network based at Queensland University of Technology.

She is a mother of one daughter, and has a granddaughter. In her spare time she meditates, paints; and plays, sings and composes music with her brothers. https://au.linkedin.com/in/tjanaragorenggoreng

Julie Szego began her career as a lawyer before switching to journalism, spending over 12 years at *The Age* newspaper. She is a freelance journalist and Fairfax columnist, writing on a wide range of social, cultural and gender issues. Her first book, *The Tainted Trial of Farah Jama*, was shortlisted for the 2015 Victorian Premier's Literary Award for Non-fiction, the 2015 Davitt Crime Writing Award for Non-fiction and the 2015 NSW Premier's Literary Award in the Multicultural category.

Disclaimer

Every care has been taken to verify names, dates and details throughout this book. But, as much is reliant on memory, some unintentional errors may have occurred. The Publisher assumes no legal liability or responsibility for inaccuracies; they do, however, welcome any information that will redress them.

A LONG WAY
FROM
NO GO

TJANARA GORENG GORENG

with Julie Szego

WILD
DINGO
PRESS

Published by Wild Dingo Press
Melbourne, Australia
books@wilddingopress.com.au
www.wilddingopress.com.au

First published by Wild Dingo Press 2018

Designer: Debra Billson
Design concept: Mandy Braddick from Womanjin Design
Original painting for book cover: Tjanara Goreng Goreng
Editor: Catherine Lewis
Printed in Australia by Griffin Press

Goreng Goreng, Tjanara, 1958-.
A long way from no go / Tjanara Goreng Goreng (author); Julie Szego (author).

A catalogue record for this
book is available from the
National Library of Australia

ISBN: 9780648215974 (paperback)
ISBN: 9780995378209 (ebook: pdf)
ISBN: 9780648215912 (eBook: ePub)

For Arika and Willa.

ACKNOWLEDGEMENTS

It's important to acknowledge the people who inspired and brought this book to fruition. To Brian James, firstly for giving the *Red Earth* to Wild Dingo Press, and Catherine Lewis for choosing to publish it as a memoir, supporting it from beginning to end with great enthusiasm and finding a fabulous writer/collaborator for me in Julie Szego. Julie, your writing of my story from hours of tapes is wonderous and brilliant, just as you are. Diamond, for always having a bed for me in Melbourne and being the best friend—our times in the desert were always the best.

To the special girlfriends in my life who loved me unconditionally and were always there for me, there are no words: Lenny, Carmen, Christie, Laura and Cousin Tanya, you are all wonderful women who gave me a reason to love myself. To Barbara Tjikatu, for being the inspiration for everything and for the cultural knowledge and unconditional love. And to Kummunarra, now in the other world, who always cared: thank you for watching over me. To My Ancestors: thank you for always being with me to face the difficulties.

I especially want to thank Dr Warwick Middleton for helping me survive, thrive and live; showing me the way to recovery and the way to manage putting priests in jail. Your knowledge, wisdom and ability as a therapist often kept me alive as you well know.

Along the roads of my life I have met some amazing souls, both women and men; to all of you I say thank you for sharing and caring, uplifting and giving to me. Special thanks to Brian Bacon for seeing who I really was and always being a good friend. To Marc for the unconditional love, and Michael for always caring. To my Tiddas in my extended community: you have always been so honest, caring and forgiving, and I'm blessed to have you all in my life—you know who you are.

Acknowledgements

I want to thank all those people in my life who gave me reasons to face adversity, who bullied me and made it hard to live—you in fact gave me the greatest gift: the desire to overcome your judgement, your cruelty and your misguided sense of who I was. I'm glad I didn't listen to you and instead chose to rise above it all; thank you for the adversity, it made me stronger. To the members of my family who never cared, I hope you read this and feel ashamed.

Most of all I want to thank the little girl who survived and chose to be a wonderful human being: Pamela Mary Williams, you are my hero.

TABLE OF CONTENTS

PROLOGUE

Few people, I suspect, can attribute a life-changing epiphany to a double-page spread in *Who* magazine. But it's thanks to that pop-culture oracle that I was jolted awake one cheerful morning in February 1995, seated at a desk by the window in the spare room of my friend's place in Glebe, the magazine flipped casually open.

Ironically, I had recently returned from India, where I spent the summer on a spiritual retreat—something I did so often you'd assume that if a blinding truth was going to strike me somewhere that would be the place. Instead I was back in Sydney, adrift, in between jobs, with no-fixed-address, crashing at my friend's while I looked for an apartment and plotted a new course, or tried to.

The double-page spread was a story about Ballarat priest Gerald Ridsdale, one of Australia's most notorious paedophiles. He indecently assaulted an altar boy during confession. He abused a boy and girl after presiding over their father's funeral. The previous year a Melbourne court sentenced Ridsdale to 18 years in prison.

Mind racing, I looked up from the page, gazed out the window. I'm pretty sure the sunlight was streaming in—but maybe that's just an affectation of memory, embroidering the moment with cliché.

And even though I was in my 40s, a mother, an Aboriginal, a public policy expert, even though, during the course of a restless and fearless life, I'd roamed the continent alone, drunk myself to oblivion, mucked in with truck drivers, mingled with Canberra's most powerful, witnessed the shocking legacy of violence against my people, battled for Indigenous rights, even changed my name to fully 'decolonise' myself, experienced profound joy and bottomless despair and confronted my demons—or so I thought—the plain message in the *Who* feature still struck me with embarrassing, almost implausible force.

All it took was the photo of that man of the cloth condemned, his depravity bared to the world.

An idea, so self-evident it's childlike, coalesced in my mind.

You mean…?

You can put them in jail?

1

GUARD OF HONOUR

To me, the row of Jacaranda trees that lined the roads between the school and town in Longreach, resembled a guard of honour—stately, graceful, distinguished, an orderly explosion of lilac. I secretly thought of the trees as my protectors, in the way kids secretly think such things.

My mum put her faith in more prosaic insurance, as adults usually do, her creed a tapestry of hard work, self-discipline, firm boundaries, devout submission. We went to church every Sunday, even in the sticky wet season. We lived in a spotless house. We always sat at the dining table during mealtimes. We always said grace before eating and the food was always plentiful and hearty. Having worked as a cook on cattle stations, mum knew how to make the kind of food men like: huge roasts, corned beef, apple pie with pastry made fresh. Impeccable Catholics to the last, on Friday nights we went down to Haddad's fish 'n chips shop. At the dinner table our conversation staples were unionism and left-wing politics—the influence of George, our father—and Catholicism.

Mum insisted we never get about town without nice clothes and nice shoes. She made me a pink and white polka dot dress with a bow at the back. When my little sister became a ballerina, mum made all her outfits too. When I attended St Joseph's Primary School—I still remember my feverish excitement on the first day—she sent me off in my freshly-ironed blue and white checked dress, panama hat and brown port (Queensland for 'case'). She taught us to sew, but if we didn't stitch proper French seams she didn't let us wear the clothes in public, even though no one could see the seams.

For a long time I thought it was disgraceful to walk around in thongs. My mother was adamant that no one would call her family, 'dirty blacks'. She would never give the authorities a reason to barge into her home and remove her children.

We were the only Aboriginal family living in Longreach, a town in central-west Queensland licked by the 'long reach' of the Thomson River, where the streets are named after birds. All my friends were white. Occasionally, another Aboriginal family washed up in town, but none stayed. One family, the Tobys, lived there for a while, their boy attending St Joseph's. But he didn't last long. He was relentlessly bullied, and soon enough, the Tobys went back to where they came from.

When I was five, a kid at school called my brother, Kevin, a 'nigger'. Kevin bashed the kid, which got him suspended. He was constantly getting suspended.

George liked to joke about white people or *migloos* as we called them. One time, waiting at a red light with several of us kids in the back, George watched a group of people traversing the only pedestrian crossing in Longreach.

He cocked his head back and grinned.

'Do you think we could run over all 'em *migloos?*'

He also used to make us laugh by claiming he was the son of an Afghan camel rider. We knew it was a lie though his skin was dark. The problem was that George Arthur Williams—for some reason I always called him George, never 'dad'—rarely talked about his background. The little I know, I gleaned as an adult from researching his family history. I discovered he was dark Irish with a sprinkling of Welsh; his ancestors arrived at Moreton Bay in 1873 on the migrant ship, the *Storm King*. His father, Jenkins Williams, moved to Charters Towers in the gold rush and married Georgina, my Irish grandmother, who worked most of her life at the presbytery of the Catholic Church to secure her son a free education at Mount Carmel Boys' School.

We knew how George and mum met—she was working in a cafe in Rockhampton, still in her teens, when one day he walked in, ten years her senior, a dashing soldier, just returned from the Second World War. In a sepia-toned photograph of him in his uniform, smoky eyes peer out from under the slouching hat.

'Do what makes you happy,' George liked to say, although at other times he pushed us to do what made *him* happy, as did mum.

She worked as a cleaner at the ANZ Bank in town. Sometimes I tagged along during her cleaning shifts. While she mopped the floors, I gorged on Arnott's biscuits in the tearoom. In the years to come, once I was at the Catholic boarding school, mum never saw a cent of her salary—it went straight to the school to pay for her children's tuition.

'If you have a talent for something then you have to let me know because it's God's will that we use our talents,' mum said. And we were undoubtedly a talented family, and a big one, me being the middle child of seven. My brother, Peter, was a jazz pianist and our granny, Beatrice, mum's mother, played too. In the evenings we stood round the piano, playing and singing together.

When I was about eight years old, Mum said to me, 'You have to choose between swimming and piano because I can't afford both'. I took some piano lessons at school, but the nun rapped me over the knuckles with a ruler; so I chose swimming.

According to family legend, when I was five, George clocked me swimming 58 seconds up a 50-metre pool. 'We have a champion,' he beamed. From that moment, George became my swimming coach and our special bond was formed. He dressed me in white togs and white tracksuits because he wanted me to stand out when I won gold.

I remember him saying to me once: 'When you've won a gold medal and you're up on that dais, make sure you shake the hand of the girls on either side. Because even though they're white, and you're doing this because we want to show them that being black is better, you never tell them that.'

George lost his father, my grandfather, Jenkins, when he was only six months old, probably in the First World War. I have very few childhood memories of his mother, my grandmother Georgina; I'm guessing she died when I was very young. In one photo she looks like a plump Irish woman, wearing glasses and one of those 1930s dresses. On one occasion in the 1970s, a brother of George's visited us with his son; and I was so shocked because they were both lily-white with blonde hair!

Mum said that 20 years later, she and George visited an estranged sister who lived in the town of Beaudesert in Queensland's Scenic Rim Region. Before this, mum had barely even heard of her. She said this sister looked exactly like him; the siblings cried; apparently, they hadn't seen each other since they were little. We don't know how they became estranged in the first place—perhaps my grandmother had been forced to give up some of her children because she couldn't afford to keep them all. But even after the siblings' tearful reunion, George maintained his silence about the past, and we didn't ever visit her again.

Otherwise, he liked noise. He furtively placed whoopee cushions round the house and when you sat on one he howled with laughter at the fart noise. When he was about to fart himself, he lifted his leg to make a performance out of it, and we would all run off, shrieking.

Georgina succeeded in getting her son through high school, but work being scarce during the Depression years, after graduation he got labouring jobs on properties in the bush and obtained a trade certificate as a machinist. He worked for the council, driving tractors and graders.

So, the George my mother stumbled upon in the cafe was battle-hardened from many theatres of conflict. We all knew he had seen service in New Guinea, but that's all we knew about his wartime experiences, at least back then. Other than his battles against the bosses, of course! George was a Communist Party veteran—he was 18 when he joined. He helped print *The Tribune*, the newspaper of the Communist Party of Australia, and hid the bundles in haystacks at Charters Towers because the cops used to chase him. And he agitated in the shearers' union.

On a more personal front, he was a fabulous dancer, and quite literally swept mum off her feet. It was when they married in 1948 that she converted to Catholicism. But this was always tempered with commonsense. After school one day I felt troubled—one of the nuns told the class that Captain Cook discovered Australia and when he arrived, there was no one here. Mum shrugged it off. 'You know what, love, the Catholics don't know everything,' she said.

And away from the townspeople, on the secluded banks of the Thomson, mum sang the songs. She never dared speak language in the town because that would risk attracting the attention of the authorities. But here, with me at her side, she was uninhibited, here she preserved the traditional knowledge her grandfather, Alick, bequeathed to her when she was little.

I heard many stories about great-grandfather Alick because my mother, born in 1929, the year of the Depression, practically lived with him until she was ten. Her mother moved around central-western Queensland, as did many Aboriginals during that time, living in humpies that resembled *gunyas*[1] with corrugated iron.

Alick was a proper law man as he had been initiated and had, himself, initiated other men. He sat around the fire with sticks, telling stories at night. In later years, mum depicted this scene in a special heirloom quilt, now hanging on a wall in my big sister's home.

During her years with Alick my mother even got to attend school. When her mother, Beatrice, took her back to live with the family in Rockhampton, mum's education abruptly stopped at age ten—a fact she related to me with sadness and a pinch of anger.

Alone together in the bush, we sang *Garin Inna Narmin*, a song that every Aboriginal in southwestern Queensland knew. And we collected bush tucker, just as she had done with Alick. She would forage for mushrooms, possums, goannas. 'We'll never starve,' she said.

'Sit by the rock over there,' she said one time, 'and if any animals come, don't move. Just sit very still.' Mum ambled further down the river, searching the scrub for tucker, disappearing from view.

A rustle of leaves. Suddenly, a goanna! I held my breath. But though I was impatient for mum to get back, I wasn't really scared. In that moment I felt a connection between the earth, the trees

---

1 *Gunyas* is the Aboriginal word for a type of house/lean-to that is built from materials available in the natural environment.

and that goanna, and I sensed a voice saying, 'You're going to be alright'. And because my mother talked about him all the time, I decided the voice belonged to my great-grandfather, Alick. My ancestors were watching over me. Along with the jacarandas.

When I was older, I told mum I wanted to learn the business. But she shook her head. 'That stuff is past now.'

2

WHITE LIES

In the late 1980s, I was attending an Aboriginal women's conference at Canberra with my daughter when an extended clan relative approached me. Searching my face, she asked, 'Who's your family? Because you look like Maureen Williams.'

'Yes, Maureen's my mother,' I replied, gratified.

It was always flattering to hear I resembled my mother, a beautiful woman with thick dark hair and red lipstick, her signature decoration.

'Right,' this relative continued, 'and her father was Clive Quinn'.

'Clive Quinn?' I exclaimed. 'Who's that?'

As far as I knew, mum's father was Wilfred Stanley, who we called Fred, supposedly a Maori with some Irish or other Anglo-Celtic blood in his lineage, and wedded to Beatrice, my grandmother. I say 'supposedly' because at that time many Aboriginal people described themselves as Maori or Indian to avoid the Aboriginal Protection Authority that forced Indigenous Australians to live on missions. Police records from 1935 from Eidsvold, a rural town north west of Brisbane, describe my mother Maureen Marva Stanley, then aged six, as one of the district's 'half castes'.

But as is the case with a great many Aboriginal families, our genealogy comes replete with white lies, so to speak: secrets and fabrications. And so, on this day I learnt that my real grandfather was not Fred Stanley after all, but Clive Quinn, the son of a full-blooded Aboriginal woman who—shockingly for the racially-segregated 1800s—lived openly with her Scottish husband, Mr Quinn, in the Queensland town of Theodore. Clive was tall, wiry and very black. A successful jockey, he was a spiffy dresser and, as my mother liked to say of Aboriginal men—for reasons I now more fully understood—utterly unreliable. As I later confirmed, my grandmother, Beatrice, had Clive's baby out of wedlock. Later on, Fred came along and became a father to my mother who took his name.

'No point marrying a black man,' mum warned me and my sisters as teenagers. 'You won't get anywhere. They won't look after you.'

Amazing how such sentiments, that only white men can be considered protectors, get under your skin, seeping into your consciousness; even when my mother's life experience blatantly contradicts them. Though to be fair, our family history reveals plenty more Fred Stanleys—white men who stepped up to the plate. Chief among them was Fitzpierce Joyce, and what I know about him comes mainly from history books and internet sites such as *Trove*. He was one of nine sons of Pierce Joyce, an Irish grazier from Mervue in County Galway, whose full brood stretched to 17, and whose lineage probably stretched back to a Norman called 'de Joss', a nobleman washed up on the isles in the wake of the Norman conquest. His descendants settled in Wales and in the 13th century, marched into Ireland. The family name mutated over the centuries as did the family crest, shedding the demi-wolf—the mongrel offspring of a dog and a wolf—for a griffin, a legendary creature, part-lion, part-eagle.

According to *The Joyces of the Overflow and Eidsvold*, a (white-washed—I'll get to that) family history written in 1961 by Kathleen Nutting, Fitz was 'six feet tall and golden-fair, magnificent as a Viking'. Ireland, Nutting writes, had become 'too small' for the towering Fitz and four of his equally large-framed and exuberant brothers, who arrived in Queensland in the late 19th century, each carrying £2000—a gift from their father. The siblings invested the money in a property in the Dalby district, and drove round in 'buggy and four-in-hand' attending race meetings in top hats, dazzling the locals.

In 1905, Fitz partnered with another Irish farmer and local politician, DeBurgh Persse, to buy Eidsvold Station, near the central Queensland gold mining town of the same name. The pair sealed the deal for this fertile tract of land on the Burnett River with the marriage of Fitz and DeBurgh's daughter, Eileen—Fitz also exchanging Catholicism for the Protestant faith in the process. The newlyweds took up residence on a property graced with two towering bottle trees. Over time this pastoral investment yielded bountiful returns. Fitz grazed sheep until spear grass and stomach worms forced a switch to cattle, and lengthy experimentation found the Hereford a more adaptable and hardier breed; the superior Hereford becoming synonymous with the station itself.

Celebrations during picnic race weeks at the township of Gayndah to the east were some of 'the most enjoyable times ever experienced on the Burnett,' Fitz reminisced in *The Brisbane Courier* in 1932. Graziers and stockmen from around the country descended on the area: 'young bloods' renting houses, with servants and chef, for weeks of feasting and merriment. One of the 'ministers of religion' declared at a banquet that he was going to get a racehorse, so he could 'join in the fun'.

Fitz personally achieved international fame by inventing an instrument for dehorning cattle. As *The Courier* also reported:

'Mr. Joyce is a firm believer in de-horning, and it is largely due to this practice that his cattle have always been sought'.

In subsequent decades, under the stewardship of Fitz's son Barney and other descendants, Eidsvold continued luring what the *Australian Dictionary of Biography* calls 'notables'—Joyce Grenfell, Dame Annabelle Rankin, Sir Zelman Cowen and Prince Richard of Gloucester—to open its annual cattle sales. The Joyces twice entertained Prince Charles, who reciprocated by inviting them to his wedding in 1981.

As I intimated earlier, the official history of Fitz Joyce omits all but the occasional breezy reference to Indigenous peoples. On 6 June 1910, a diary entry recording his lengthy double-buggy and four-in-hand journey to Gayndah sixty miles away, notes: 'Wag with me'—Wag being described in the family history as 'a young halfcaste stockman'. Otherwise, blackfellas make only an oblique appearance through the blackface routines of Fitz's much-loved bachelor brother, Patrick, Eidsvold's versatile bookkeeper who 'could handle anything from cooking a five-course dinner to performing a corroboree'.

'Visitors to Eidsvold always hoped that they might see a corroboree,' writes Nutting in the family history, 'but though there were plenty of aborigines, they were subject to fits of shyness and often unwilling to perform. With Uncle Pat, blackened and done out in war-paint and gum leaves, to lead them, their confidence returned. Nothing could be less like the hard, lean aboriginal-type than was huge Uncle Pat, but in his shaking at the knees and chanting of native songs he equalled any one of them!'

In truth, Fitz enjoyed intimate bonds with the region's 'plenty aborigines'; one in particular, a woman. While her name does not appear on official records from the time, she is a revered subject in my family's oral history. During a period in the late 1800s, well before he bought Eidsvold, Fitz ran Hawkwood station further north, home to staghounds, dingo hunts and '600 well-bred horses on the run'. While there, he became romantically involved with an Aboriginal woman from the Wulli Wulli tribe: Grace, my maternal ancestor.

The couple had a daughter called Frances or Fanny. As with Clive Quinn's full-blood Aboriginal mother and her Scottish partner, the relationship between Grace and Fitz, a prominent landowner, was unusual for the times. Mum reckons Fitz must have really loved Grace because he gave her a house on one of his stations and looked after her until she died.

An old white lady, a descendent from Fitz and Eileen, had a lot of historical documents and records about Grace, but for years and years she refused to give them to mum. So there is a history of silence and cover-up in the white family. We, on the other hand, claim Grace and Frances proudly as our own.

Mum has alluded to the existence of documents that show Fitz actually married Grace. Is this tender story of genuine and courageous interracial love reality or mythology, or a bit of both? It's impossible to know. What I do know, what I've come to learn, is that colonisation, including sexual violence carried out by white men against black women, bequeathed a legacy of shame for the victims and their descendants. Sometimes Indigenous peoples compensate for that shame by inventing fairytales, doing some whitewashing of their own.

In the late 1800s, a seven-year-old Aboriginal boy turned up at Eidsvold station. As I understand the story, the young descendent of the Wakka Wakka people, from nearby Ban Ban Springs, had fled a massacre and spent years lost, just roaming about the region and living off the land in any way he could. This sketchy account comes from my mother, but she persistently declined to go into detail about the massacre or how this boy, her grandfather Alick, came to be wandering outback Queensland alone.

Fitz took him in and named him Alick Little. Alick worked hard, stocking horses, shearing sheep, growing vegetables. He learnt English, grew into a sturdy and wily adult and fell in love with the stationmaster's Aboriginal daughter, Frances, roughly the same age as him. Although Fitz had wanted to send Frances to the family in Ireland so she could obtain an English education and be a proper Miss, he gave the couple his blessing—after all, Alick had worked on the station forever, and the family trusted him. Together, Alick and Frances spoke the Wakka Wakka and Wulli Wulli languages.

At a memorable and emotional Native Title Gathering in Gayndah in 2015, my cousins, elder brother and I drove to Eidsvold Station to see where Alick and our relatives had worked and lived.

'This is our country,' I said as we drove up to the big house and around, noting the small slab timber hut where we were told Alick had lived. My cousin was worried: 'Are you sure we should be doing this?' I pressed the accelerator and careened around the homestead. Seeing nobody was home, we explored the station. I had an eerie feeling of spirits of our Ancestors in that place, the fact that it was deserted made it even more so. I could sense Alick and everyone else who had lived and worked there as we drove around.

Fitz arranged for Alick to obtain an exemption under Queensland law so he would not be removed to the missions; and my great-grandfather always carried his exemption pass around in case he needed to produce it on demand. Which is not to say he was a meek Uncle Tom.

Alick also figured out that if he was able to support his family, he could wrangle his freedom. He set up camp on the outskirts of a number of towns and established market gardens and sold fruit and vegetables to white folks; and he made sure that any of his children who worked for station owners got paid their rightful wages.

Alick Little is 'a cunning and clever man', noted a bureaucrat in Queensland's Department of Aboriginal Affairs—adding that the authorities must be on their guard with him because he 'knows his rights'. Indeed, the Eidsvold Police Letterbooks from 1935 to 1956 tell us Alick was, as we say, 'known to authorities'. On 15 May 1935, he was convicted for allegedly 'wilfully destroying the house of Flossy Perkins at Eidsvold'. Perkins was another Aboriginal woman who worked on the station, but that's all the light I can shed on this police note. The next day, he was 'in jail'. A week later, the notation, carrying a hint of exasperation reads: 'Suggest Alick Little be sent to a settlement'. Two months later, 'Alick Little and family moved to Dawson in order to not be forced onto the mission and have his pass revoked.

I think my grandmother, Beatrice, sent mum to Alick because he was safe and constant, and based near Eidsvold station. Mum told me her parents' house in Rockhampton, on the other hand, was always full of drunks—but I don't know if that's just her prejudice. I know she used to have to go on long errands on foot to get milk for the family. By that stage, her mother was married to Fred, and more children had come along. There were 12 years, and five brothers, between my mother and her little sister Ruby. My aunt Ruby described a happy childhood but of course she was much younger than mum, who found herself burdened with raising siblings when she rejoined her family. Beatrice, at least, seemed appreciative of mum's labour, and would berate Ruby saying, 'why can't you be more like your big sister?'

When Beatrice and Fred moved to Rockhampton, life improved in terms of income. A stockman and a drover, Fred found a lot of work in western Queensland. The boys, my uncles, also worked as shearers and drovers, and were very spiffy—at that time Aboriginal men dressed like African-Americans, thanks to the influence of the US soldiers based in the area during the war. The men would wear hats and smart clothes for the local dances, as did the women. Mum and her sisters preened in the latest fashions, going to great lengths to be accepted into white culture; very early on, my mother decided she was going to have a better life than her mother—a white person's life.

As mum told me, she left home at 16, just six years after coming back to live with Beatrice and Stanley. She'd landed a job in a cafe as a cook, so moved into a room at a boarding house down the road. Wearing her hair long and her signature red lipstick, she looked an immaculate picture of beauty and, as it happened, enjoyed only a fleeting period of freedom, because one day a dashing soldier walked into the cafe.

When she met and married my father, they moved more than 600 kilometres inland from the coast near Rockhampton, to the Longreach area, where they lived on a cattle station. My brother, Peter, was born there two years after the wedding. I arrived eight years later, and was christened Pamela Mary Williams—a name I have since disowned.

For the first few years, dad was building the family home on the edge of Longreach in Spoonbill Street—the streets running east-west are named after water birds; those running north-south, after land birds. During this time, mum saved money by living in a tent with us first four children on the cattle and sheep station, 35 kilometres north-west, off the Longreach to Winton Road. While dad earnt money building fences with a contractor, mum looked after goats so we had fresh milk.

That cattle station where I spent my first years still exists—flat, expansive; the earth blazing gold and pink. It boasts an historic homestead from the 1800s, and a tantalising link with notoriety.

The property, I recently learnt, bears the ruins of the stockyard said to be used by the stockman, drover and cattle thief, Harry Redford, who was the inspiration for Captain Starlight in Rolf Boldrewood's 19th-century novel, *Robbery Under Arms*. Redford stole about 1000 cattle from a station near Longreach, and apparently held them in these stockyards before driving them for an epic three months and nearly 1300 kilometres through the Strzelecki Desert to South Australia; along the same track Burke and Wills had embarked on roughly 10 years earlier and perished. The Law finally caught up with Redford in New South Wales in 1872, but when he faced trial in Queensland, the jury was so dazzled with his cross-country dash, they found him not guilty.

The station's name has an otherworldly, eerie ring: *No Go*. But *No Go*'s romantic associations were lost on my mother, who remembered her days there as tough and bitter. George took to drinking over-proof rum. And he took to hitting her.

One night, mum whacked him back.

'If you ever do that again, I'm gone,' she hissed.

Then she laid down the rules that would keep the family safe and together—at least in our home: 'You're not drinking like that anymore. You're drinking one bottle a day, and I'm in charge of the money.' And with that, she took control of his money, doling out rations for gambling on the races and for one bottle of beer a day, which he drank down by the river.

He never hit her again.

When I was about four we moved into the house that dad built in Longreach as mum and George decided we'd get a better education in the town, and by then, George had got a permanent job with the Longreach City Council. We often joked about how George built the place from materials that fell off a truck during his work for the council.

Another reason why George wanted to leave No Go Station and move the family to Longreach was to escape mum's Aboriginal relatives who were scattered between Winton and Rockhampton. It wasn't that he didn't respect her Indigenous heritage; quite the opposite, in fact. He simply refused to tolerate the idea of the extended clan descending on our home, which was indeed the done thing in those days.

'I'm not having the whole family living in the house,' he spat. He especially hated Uncle Tibby—an extended clan relative— turning up and demanding to sleep at the house. I don't think mum wanted him around either. A drover who never married, Tibby had wandering hands.

On a few occasions, Tibby stood at our front gate and yelled for mum, using her traditional name.

'Mooki!'

Silence.

'Mooki!'

We scrambled for cover, scared out of our wits. George emerged from the house and confronted him.

'What do you want, Tibby?' he growled.

'I wanna sleep. Sleep in the shed.'

'Nah. Go downtown.'

George later explained that he simply couldn't abide immorality or wrongdoing. As I found out only once I was an adult, he refused to have anything to do with mum's biological father, Clive Quinn, either, because he had done something bad to a young Aboriginal woman. George had even got into a fist fight with Clive over the scandal.

'You must have nothing more to do with him,' George said to mum. Which is why us children never knew about the spiffy-looking jockey who was our real grandfather.

3

THE SHARK

About a year after we moved to Longreach, George got a job at the showgrounds, working as the showground keeper for the council, so we moved to a house on the site. Under his care, the grounds soon bloomed with wattle trees, and vegetables sprouted from the soil.

Possessing a restless entrepreneurial spirit, however, George recruited all us kids to his various schemes at this time. Whatever he could sell, he would. We gathered rolls of newspapers and he sold them to the butcher. On the weekends he earned extra cash washing football jerseys, and the boys sold cans and had paper runs.

He also loved tinkering with cars. With his sheep dog Wanni by his side, George would wile away the hours after work and on the weekends. We had one of those good-looking Fords, then one of those Holdens with the silver bits jutting out the front, then the combi van. Wanni died from pneumonia after being out in the rain one night—it was the only time I saw my father really upset.

When we moved to Rockhampton during my teens, George and I would take to the dirt roads in the purple dawn, before the searing heat settled in, feeling the peace of it, listening to the birds calling.

From the time George became convinced I was a swimming champion when I dazzled him with the stopwatch in the pool at age five—about a year after we'd moved off the station and into town—he persisted in the role of coach. Mum said that he probably saw a chance to fulfil his own childhood dreams because apparently, he was also a strong swimmer at his boys' school and had aspired to medals.

We would rise early while my mother and siblings were still asleep and the streets outside empty. In the weak morning light, we would drive around the corner to our local pool. On these mornings, he made me swim one mile—60 laps of a 50-metre pool—and after school I swam another 60 laps and lifted weights. He was training me to be a 50-metre sprinter. His abiding piece of advice that I always thought about when I was racing was: 'For the last 15 metres, you have to pretend there's a shark behind you'.

It was at about the same age, around the time we moved to the showgrounds, that I started developing sleeping problems. I couldn't doze off unless I rocked and sang myself to sleep, so I would rock and sing the songs I had heard on the radio. But even after I fell asleep I would make loud moaning noises. This infuriated George. He would lock me in the outside laundry where I would sleep on the canvas camp bed with Ringo, our black-and-white kelpie. I knew it was George who insisted that I sleep outside; mum was upset but she wouldn't stand up to him because he was the one who had to go to work the next day. I remember crouching on the back-door step crying, terrified. This went on for ages—I can't recall how long. Of all us kids,

I alone got to see the flip-side of George—his dark, occasionally cruel and devastatingly enigmatic side.

The presbytery at Longreach was familiar territory for our family. Akin to a community centre, with the kindergarten next-door and the primary school down the road, we often milled about the presbytery, and the church and Convent. I was also familiar with the priests, especially one called Father Mick Hayes who spearheaded the Rockhampton diocese involvement in the Aboriginal ministry.

Hailing from the Dawson River town of Theodore, Hayes was a tall, slim and fine-looking man; people compared him to a racehorse, and he was as strong as one. He had a notoriously firm grip and liked to grab women at will, squeezing them into a bear hug, while kissing them. Even older women such as my mother weren't immune from his exuberant physicality.

As a six-year-old, my father began to take me alone with him to the presbytery; and so he did this one fateful day in 1964. I was wearing the pink and white polka dot dress my mother had made me. Father Hayes was there, and he introduced my father to another priest who I now know was Father Grove Johnson: a thin, spectacled, ginger-haired man in his late 40s or early 50s. He wore the regulation black pants with a white shirt and two gold crosses on his collar. As I discovered in the years that followed, Father Johnson always wore his uniform.

George drank a cup of tea with the two men in the dining room while I waited on a chair in the hallway. A short time later my father came out and said he would pick me up in a couple of hours. I have no idea why George left me there, but nor was this a big deal; as I said, the presbytery was like a second home and Father Hayes, hardly a stranger to me. He took my hand and led me to the kitchen, where he gave me a glass of home-made lemonade. Then he took me down the hallway and into a room with a brown cupboard, a desk and a single bed. It was not unusual; I had played in this room before. The man with the gold crosses on each side of his shirt was waiting there, seated at the desk. He put me on a chair next to him and said he wanted to show me something, to play a game.

Father Hayes left, shutting the door behind him. I turned to watch him leave. What's going on? I wondered. I turned back to the man with the gold crosses. He was holding up a fob watch which he began swinging back and forth.

'Just watch the watch swinging,' he said in a sing-song voice. I lost awareness of what was going on and can now only assume I was hypnotised or lost consciousness.

My dress was pulled up around my waist. A heavy load on the right side of my body. He was lying on top of me. He rolled around, rubbed himself hard against me, touched me, did what I sensed as weird things. He produced the fob watch again, sang again.

'You go back to sleep.'

I was alone in the room. The watch was on the table. The door was open. I got up from the bed and went down the hallway to the kitchen. George was there with Father Hayes and the man with the gold crosses.

'I've come to get you,' George said.

I felt sore between my legs. George took my hand in his and we went home, saying nothing.

'Each time you win a race you can have a Drumstick,' George said, as I lowered my frame into the pool. So, I won my races, powering through the water like there was a shark behind me. Afterwards, I devoured my Drumstick.

Father Grove Johnson visited Longreach a handful of times before I was nine. Several times George took me to the presbytery and left me there; each time I grew more fearful. I thought: this priest is not a kind man, even if he plays at being friendly. He gave me altar wine. I sipped from the cup. The wine took effect and I often dosed off. One time I found myself in a smaller room with a single bed and a window with green and yellow curtains, a large desk and two chairs, a black jacket draped over one of them.

His rough weight on me. His body rubbing against me. Something wet and horrible on my leg. During one such encounter, he said: 'If you talk about this, then you'll have to kill yourself'.

From around the age of five years, I was in and out of hospital with urinary tract infections. Sitting at the edge of a hospital bed, the nurses hovered around and poked at me, my mum and sisters came for a visit. White blisters and boils appeared on my buttocks and genitals. Mum took me to our family doctor, a man we called 'Doctor Tom'. He produced the sharpened end of a matchstick.

'Look here,' he instructed mum, pointing at one of the blisters. 'Burst them like this.'

I winced over and over. This was the extent of his advice: pop the blisters and boils, and put some cream on.

Alone one day with mum, I lingered, trying to find a silence in our daily routine. A voice prodded me: 'Tell her'. I trembled softly. I opened my mouth, I stammered something. But mum's head was elsewhere, she was always rushing around, rarely listening.

The moment passed.

When I was around 10 or 11, I started to get rebellious about swimming. George was no longer coaching me, and we had a new coach.

'Watch out for him,' the other girls warned me, confessing he liked to touch their pre-pubescent bodies. I was nervous about this coach doing the same to me, although by this stage I had learnt how to keep out of people's way. All the same, I disliked him. One day he pissed me off so much that I stormed off from the pool in a rage and walked all the way home.

'Unless you get me a new coach I'm not going back to swimming,' I announced to my parents.

'No,' George said, 'you've got to be a champion and be above whatever's going on. If the coach is making you mad, just get in the pool and swim it off.'

You're the one making me mad, I thought to myself. Why the hell am I doing all this training, collecting all these medals, making everyone happy when I'm bloody miserable?

I picked up playing the piano around this time and kept on with swimming training, realising I didn't have a choice—what George said happened; I had no say in it.

I was still singing and groaning in my sleep when I was 10 years old, but I was allowed to sleep in a room with my sister when she came home from boarding school. When she was away, though, George would come in and hit me, trying to get me to be quiet. Eventually my parents slipped me some sleeping pills; and thus a habit was formed early in life.

I am 11. There's a swimming meet in Rockhampton. Afterwards George takes me to the presbytery, the Bishop's house, a sprawling mansion across the road from the cathedral. It is lunchtime—or maybe tea time?—people mill around the dining room, the clink of cutlery, the low hum of voices.

Father Mick Hayes.

A winding heavy staircase: a long hallway with rooms to the side. Two flights of stairs, Father Hayes yanks me close.

The room with the tall ceiling, the desk, the chairs, the single bed.

Father Grove Johnson.

The locked door. The open door.

The locked door again.

4

'LISTEN TO GOD'

Nestled in the foothills of Athelstane Range in west Rockhampton is the suburb aptly named, The Range, and Agnes Street, which traces the mountain ridge. Here, a gentle breeze provides some relief against the Queensland heat, and expansive views take in the lower plain of the Fitzroy River. It was to here that in 1895 the order of the Sisters of Mercy—who, needless to say, we schoolgirls called 'the Sisters of No Mercy'—shifted the school and convent that became known as The Range Convent and High School; one of a cluster of deliberately imposing buildings with timber towers, brick dormitories, arched windows and sprawling verandahs.

And it was here, aged 12 going on 13, that I started boarding school.

I had wanted to join my older sister, Patricia, at her convent school in Brisbane, but mum said, 'We've got plans to move to Rocky (Rockhampton), so you're going to school there'; and the convent took me in because I was a swimming champion. Still, I was pleased there was another girl from my class in Longreach heading to the same school. As the summer holidays drew to a close, anticipation overtook me.

The journey to Rockhampton was exciting and romantic. Dressed in my new uniform, I boarded the sleeper carriage in the old, clattering train for the roughly 500-kilometre overnight journey, and sank into the beautiful leather seats. For years I had watched my three older siblings head off to boarding school by themselves: Patsy to Brisbane by plane, Peter and Bub (Kevin) down the road to Yeppoon by train. Now it was my turn to be brave.

Arriving at Agnes Street, I walked through the gates of the sprawling complex. To the left, I saw the convent, a timber building with the chapel at the south end. On the right I came to the boarding house, Genazzano, a three-storey rectangular brick building, with a corrugated-iron gabled roof, surrounded by brick arched verandahs. When I ventured inside to the dormitory I found a double row of beds; and on the verandah in the far corner, was the nun's room with four beds next to it.

I was assigned to a bed out on the verandah, near the nuns. The nuns explained it was best I slept on the verandah given I had swimming training early in the morning, so I could slip out with the coach, without waking the other girls. (In an unusual honour for a child of my age I had gone straight to being captain of the swimming team.)

Years later at a high school reunion, one of those other girls, Maryanne, confessed she had complained to the nuns that she didn't want to sleep in the same dormitory as 'a black', and that that was the real reason the nuns put me out on the verandah.

It was true that Maryanne occasionally lashed out and called me an 'Abo', but in primary school I'd learnt not to retaliate against such insults because, in the event of a fight, I'd be the one punished—never the white kid. And my mum continued to warn us that if we, as Aboriginal kids, ever misbehaved at school, the authorities could take away our right to an education for good.

Anyway, I was grateful for my private space on the verandah. After early morning training, I would return to school and eat breakfast on my own—the others having already eaten—before running up to class. Homesick, I would often sit on my bed looking out at the hills and the Fitzroy River, with Gracemere and Longreach shimmering in the distance, thinking about my big sister away at school in Brisbane, wishing I could be with her, or at least back home with my mother.

On the first Sunday, one of the nuns took us to a classroom in the school building and told us to sit at the desks. She wrote the names of the boarders in chalk on the blackboard then wrote a sample letter from a boarder to their parents.

'Now all of you write this same letter to your parents,' the nun instructed us. The letter said that school was wonderful, we were loving our studies and we weren't homesick. I was horrified. I was actually terribly homesick, but now I was forbidden from confessing my true feelings to my parents. On that Sunday we all dutifully wrote the same letter home. And in the years that followed, I kept my heartache and longing a secret.

Most of the nuns were total bitches. There was only one truly nice nun, Sister Mercedes, who came when I was in Year 9. She was the second piano teacher. The first piano teacher was a cranky old thing who would get annoyed with me for sitting down to play outside hours, even though there was no one around. But Sister Mercedes let me come in and play once the other girls had done their practice.

And there was Sister Marie, who played the guitar at Mass. I was desperate to learn guitar, but my mother couldn't afford to sign me up for lessons. But I kept begging my parents to at least get me a guitar, and eventually, George got one off my uncle. After that, while Sister Marie was teaching the other students,

I sat up the back and watched—which, to her credit, she let me do. So I learned how to play guitar too.

There was also an eccentric and rather cute, elderly French nun, Sister Valerian, who wore one of those old-fashioned habits, black and plastered over the forehead. Another nun, whose name I've forgotten, was tiny, four-foot nothing and we reckoned, really old, probably in her eighties. During mealtimes in the dining room, she paced up and down, inspecting our progress, while reading a Mills and Boon.

But as I said, one nun was mean and a bit shifty. Sister Jean-Marie had a tight and tired face. She'd take every opportunity to denigrate me in front of the other girls, saying something about me being black and not very smart or capable. Also, we all thought she was a lesbian. Every night, one Year 11 student—a plump, mature-looking blonde who would flick her hair back like Marilyn Monroe, disappeared into Sister Jean-Marie's room, closing the door behind her. The two of them stayed in the room for hours and hours. 'They're lesbians,' the rest of us would snigger.

When I arrived at boarding school I was the only Aboriginal student other than my friend Margaret Smith, who came up as a day student. Margaret's mother used to live on the same cattle property as mum. Later on, a couple of Aboriginal girls came from St Joseph's Neerkol Orphanage past Gracemere. They were real sad-looking girls. One of them, Wanda, was tall and very dark. I don't know how they ended up at the orphanage—whether they were taken from their families or abandoned by them. We now know, from two official inquiries, that the vulnerable children at Neerkol were subjected to unspeakable physical and sexual abuse for decades until its closure in 1978.

Then, in my second year at the convent, a bunch of girls arrived from Palm Island. We had some fun with them and orchestrated ritual pranks: short-sheeting every new girl's bed so she got all tangled, that sort of thing. One night we sat out on the verandah until late, telling ghost stories. Afterwards we dressed up in black and crept over to the other sleeping girls, spooking them. They woke, shrieking in terror and yelled for the nuns, while we culprits rushed into our beds and lay there, all innocent.

When the girls from Palm Island and other missions arrived, the nuns decided on a social experiment: they housed all these Aboriginal girls, including me, in a renovated section of the basement of the building. The nuns thought they were doing us a good deed; they assumed 'the mission girls' would want to live together and that if they all shared the same space for a year they could then assimilate into ordinary dormitory life. My role was to mentor the black girls because—as the nuns put it— I was 'used to being around white people'. The white girls, on the other hand, were jealous because we had our own kitchen and washing machine. Little did they know we had to walk down a dark staircase to reach our quarters which particularly freaked out all the mission girls. It freaked them out so much I reckon that's why six months later every last one of them had run away. We never heard from these girls again.

Boarding school had its moments of fun and camaraderie as I collected some diverse friends. There was a Chinese girl whose parents owned the local Chinese restaurant; she was a clever spark, good at physics and chemistry. There was also Jeannie, a real wild thing. And Carmel from west Rockhampton whose mother used to foster Aboriginal kids, at times having 15 kids under her roof. My best friend, Heidi, was a German girl. Her father managed a hotel in Fiji. She seemed so exotic, spending her summer holidays in that tropical paradise. Some of the girls would go to Fiji with her and stay at her parents' resort, but of course we never had the money for me to do that.

On one occasion, Heidi somehow managed to get hold of a key to the convent, which was behind the chapel across the driveway. In the middle of the night we decided to spy on the nuns. Like the boarding house, the nunnery had a wide verandah wrapped around its corridors and rooms through which you could access the chapel. Creeping out of the dormitory, we tip-toed into the chapel. Needless to say there was nothing much to see! But we thought it was a wild adventure: it was such a thrill to prowl around in the dark.

In 1971, the same year I started boarding school, my parents moved to Rockhampton just as they had foreshadowed. George got a job at the hospital as a wardsman in the geriatric ward, a job he held until he retired many years later. They moved into a house in the town's west on a main street not far from the airport and just down the hill from my school. In September during the second school holidays, I moved in for the first time. It was a pleasant, plain timber cottage: three bedrooms with a big double-storey sleepout on the side. As usual, George made sure the paint never peeled and the garden always bloomed. Still, I was used to hanging round with a lot of rich girls at boarding school, so for the first time I thought, 'We're rather poor'; and at the time I didn't even know the cottage was provided by the Department of Aboriginal and Islander Affairs. I thought I was coming home for good, so I was shocked when towards the end of the school holidays mum told me I'd be returning to boarding school.

'Why?' I whined. 'You live just down the road.'

'Your father wants you to stay at boarding school so you can focus and concentrate.'

Actually, it was hard to concentrate at home because I sensed things weren't right between my parents, now aged in their 40s and 50s. Until this point their relationship had seemed normal; the only tension I ever detected was after George joined the local cricket team—mum grumbled that he was travelling too much for cricket.

But now I arrived home for the weekends on a Friday night only to find them yelling at one another in the kitchen. I would decamp to mum's bedroom with my three younger siblings, James, Traci and Su Anne. We'd lock the door, play our guitars together and sing, to block out the noise. By Saturday afternoons, I had had enough and went back to school, abandoning my poor little brother and sisters, who were forced to put up with the hostilities all the time.

Eventually, mum banished George from the bedroom to the verandah in the back; and took tablets to calm herself. As for George, his colleagues at the hospital loved him as a happy-go-lucky joker—a fact that became clear to me a few years later when I started working in the wards during summer holidays. At home, though, his mood would shift and darken. He was always on a short fuse. At night we would hear him scream in his sleep.

'I dream about the war,' he said to me once. I didn't understand of course, knowing nothing of war and its effects, but I didn't like what was happening to my parents, estranged, as they were becoming: my mother distant, taking pills to calm her nerves, and he telling her she was 'a dog', in front of us kids, and yelling all the time.

At 12, while competing in the regional swimming championships, I had a breakdown of my own. To clinch the trophy as regional champion I had to swim the 100-metres freestyle. I sat on the grassy hill waiting for the race to start, exhausted from having already contested the medley, relay and backstroke. I seemed to be always in a state of perpetual weariness during that year; the relentless training, the growing pains. I faded.

'You're not there!' Mum was yelling in my ear. 'The race is about to start and you're not there!'

Groggy, I thought—not for the first time—'you can all get nicked'.

But I loved learning; I loved beating everyone to come top of the class, just as mum expected of us. While I hated maths and science, I loved English and history, French and music, and most of all, religion. I probed Buddhism and Islam, feeling my mind broaden beyond Christianity. Sometimes the nuns told us to go out and sit under the trees. 'Be still and quiet,' they said. 'Listen to God.'

I really like the quiet and stillness of the bush, and always felt there was something watching over me. It made me feel safe, loved and protected. Sitting talking to Biaime, as we called God, came easily to me. I found it curious that the nuns felt that too. Evidently, God came in many disguises.

We had to go to church every morning dressed in our uniforms and veils. My punishment whenever I did something wrong, usually something minor like not cleaning my cupboard properly, was to kneel on the marble in the chapel at night. You would have to stay there until a nun came to collect you. It was cold. My knees got sore; and like the night when Heidi and I went prowling, the chapel was all shadows except for the little light in the tabernacle that said, 'God is here'. I was terrified kneeling in the darkness, with the creaks and sighs of the old building settling. I always felt as if people or the dead spirits were around watching me. But despite my treatment at the hands of God's representatives, I had quite a good relationship with Him in those days: talking to Him a lot, begging Him to keep me safe from this bloody nun or whatever. Alone in the chapel, I felt the same peace I had experienced in the bush with mum when I felt the presence of my great-grandfather and ancestors; it felt as if there were no physical boundaries in my world, a sensation of floating up to the stars.

5

'BE CAREFUL AROUND BOYS'

My periods started; heavy, painful and embarrassing. I scrunched up my blood-stained underwear and hid them, planning to rinse them all one night when no one was around.

One day Sister Jean-Marie was roaming the dormitories, carrying out random cupboard inspections, with a bunch of girls trailing her. She arrived in my room on the verandah and began rifling through my cupboard which is when she spotted my secret pile of underwear stashed beneath some neatly folded T-shirts. She ushered the other girls in front of her so they could better see me.

'Look at this dirty black girl,' she sneered.

She ordered me to scrunch the undies up in a ball. With all eyes on me I clutched the soiled pants to my chest.

'Now, don't you know you're supposed to wash those every Sunday, like all the other girls do?' Sister Jean-Marie grabbed me by the shoulders, shoved me towards the door and pointed down the verandah in the direction of the laundry. I pushed past the dormitory spectators, eyes downcast, as anger battled humiliation. I just wanted to fall through the floor.

When mum found out I had started bleeding, she sat me down one weekend.

'You be careful now,' she said. 'Always wear your underwear and bra. And be careful around boys.'

I guess she also gave me an Aboriginal talk; about relationships, about babies being sacred, little spirit things, about modesty, about girls and women being in control of their bodies.

***

For me, adolescence coincided with an awakening Aboriginal consciousness. In Queensland in the 1970s, the natural object of our discontent was the Premier, Joh Bjelke-Petersen. 'Joh', as he was known, had a highly paternalistic approach to Aboriginal affairs, believing he knew what was good for them. He sparked controversy with his decision to block the proposed sale of a pastoral property on the Cape York Peninsula to Aboriginal people, and for granting a long-term mining lease, with favourable conditions, over vast tracks of Indigenous land in far north Queensland.

It was at this time that I started paying attention when our Elders spoke about the hardships and humiliations of the past. Sometimes we drove about two hours west from Rockhampton to the Woorabinda Aboriginal mission where some of mum's distant relatives lived; I saw for myself the poverty and subjugation Aboriginal people were experiencing and thought then, 'this is bloody awful'.

And at this time, in the 1970s, the Catholic Church became active in the fight for Aboriginal rights. This was the decade following the revolutionary Second Vatican Council, Vatican II, when missionaries were encouraged to respect and even promote local and Indigenous customs that did not contradict Catholic doctrine. That meant putting Aboriginal symbology in the Mass, including Aboriginal people, their language, songs and rituals like smoking ceremonies into Catholic rituals. They were also enthusiastic to have us contribute in this way and encourage the community to be involved in the liturgy. The priests at the Rockhampton and Townsville Diocese helped form the Queensland chapter of the Aboriginal and Torres Strait Islander Catholic Council, which every January held a conference at St. Brendan's College in Yeppoon.

When an Aboriginal housing company got started in Rockhampton, my mother and I got involved. How could we not? Whenever we went down to Vinnies to buy our second-hand clothes, we saw dozens of Aboriginal people sitting under the trees on the riverbank: we knew they had no homes, no jobs, and were drinking themselves to death.

Me and my Aboriginal school friend, Margaret, were considered rarities because in those days few Indigenous kids went to high school, so everyone encouraged us to sign on to the cause. On the weekends, Father Hayes sometimes drove us to Mackay or Townsville for Council meetings, which we found thrilling. On week nights he took us to the Bishop's house in Rocky to type up Council documents and help with admin. One evening we were so busy at the bishop's house that it was 11.30 by the time I got back to the dormitory. Sister Anne-Marie, a lovely Lebanese nun, scolded Mick Hayes, threatening, 'This girl isn't going out anymore'. So, these priests didn't have access to me anymore and I didn't have to go down to the Bishop's House late at night. It didn't mean it completely stopped though; they always found a way.

In January 1972, I was in Year 9 and the Council conference drew busloads of Aboriginals from down south. This was a huge eye-opener for me. We heard speeches from Aboriginal people involved in the negotiations with the government about mining leases in the Cape, we also heard horrific stories about the quasi-apartheid segregation on the Cape. One very old lady, with very white hair and a beautiful serene face, had come down from the far north with her people. She sat under a tree and told us stories.

'In the middle of the night the police came with dogs,' she said of the razing of Mapoon. 'They stuck us in boats, took us miles up the coast to Bamaga, up the top of Cape York, to land that wasn't ours.'

I listened to speeches from Mum Shirl and Pat Dodson, who was then a seminarian. They were electrifying. Margaret and I soaked in the heightened atmosphere, and at Mass, sang with extra gusto.

We heard testimony from Aboriginals on Palm Island about the horrendous conditions there: disease, police brutality, men dying in jail. We heard anecdotes about how Queensland's notorious Director of Aboriginal Affairs, 'Pat' Killoran, treated Aboriginal people with contempt; people would travel long distances to see him and he would keep them waiting all day, then refuse to meet them. None of which was surprising considering Killoran distinguished himself for opposing the payment of award wages to Aboriginal workers, and helped remove Aboriginal children from their parents and oversaw the police raid on the tiny Aboriginal community at Mapoon, on the Cape York Peninsula, in November 1963, when people were transported 200 kilometres from the mission to form a new community, 'New Mapoon'. The Bjelke-Peterson government had given a mining lease to an international bauxite mining company and the people were in the way. Families were forced from their homes at gunpoint and then watched as their humble dwellings were burned to the ground.

And it was at this conference, when I was about 13, that I first came across Father Leo Wright. A solid man, thirty-something, with shoulder-length black hair and a trim beard, Father Hayes and another priest, Father Mick Peters, were in the Townsville Diocese. After this conference, Father Wright seemed to turn up everywhere—at every land rights event, at every Council meeting, whether regional or state. His face was frequently in the media. He came to our weekends away with Father Hayes and often popped round for visits at my parents' house. And he would accompany Margaret and I to the photocopying room at St Brendan's College, showing us where everything was.

'Do you have everything you need?' he would ask. If there was a problem, Father Wright would know how to fix it. He was the 'go-to' man with a charismatic smile.

One night my mother came into the photocopying room, to find Margaret and I busy with our admin tasks, and Leo Wright hovering around us. No one else in the room, just us three. On seeing this, mum stormed in, grabbed my arm and hustled me out the door.

'You're coming with me,' she muttered, teeth clenched.

As we were leaving, she turned around and said something to Father Wright. I couldn't hear what she said, but her tone was clipped. She all but shoved me down the stairs. Why was she so angry, I wondered. Of course, I don't wonder now, but mum never acknowledged the source of her reaction that night. Not even when I raised the incident with her 20 years later.

When I was 14, mum decided I wouldn't be doing any more swimming. Despite my occasional resentment, even intense resentment, against swimming in the intervening years, I was now heading for the Commonwealth Games and dreamed of glory.

'No, your education is more important,' was mum's edict.

George was heartbroken. As for me, I didn't talk to her for years. So, I took up trampolining, instead, and became a champion at that. The nuns organised for three trampolines to be built on the terraced section of Genezzano down near the school and recruited a coach from the YWCA. I used go down to the YWCA trampoline by the river and practise there. Fastening the belt around my waist, I'd power through the air, double-flipping, leaping, reaching high, taking flight from the world around me and showing off my skill. I loved winning and I really loved being able to perfect something. My coach was very encouraging, and I learnt fast.

In the year I turned 15, the Council established a youth wing, and at our annual conference in Yeppoon, my Aboriginal peers elected me president. One of my first jobs was addressing the assembled bishops and Aboriginal community members. I talked about racism, the racism I experienced at school and how I was reeling from hearing the stories of Mrs Jimmy and the accounts of Aboriginal people who lived on missions with no control over their lives. I urged the bishops to confront the Queensland government about the quasi-apartheid system under which we all suffered; and with the naiveté of a teenager I fully expected them to take up the challenge.

'When I look in the mirror I see Pamela Mary Williams—not an Aboriginal girl with black skin,' I declared from the lectern.

The bishops clapped politely. Sitting alongside them in the front rows of the audience, I noticed my Elders—proud and dignified men and women—nodding at me with approval.

The following February in 1973, the Vatican's high-ranking Cardinal Karol Wojtyla, who became Pope John Paul II five years later, visited Melbourne for the 40th International Eucharistic Congress. My parents gave me permission to join the bus pilgrimage south because some older Torres Strait Islander ladies they knew were also going. Margaret was coming too. We boarded the bus, chattering with excitement.

Daylight faded, dusk arrived. I sat curled against the window in the bus as it travelled the seemingly interminable kilometres to

Canberra, en route to Melbourne. 'Where are we now?' I wondered. It grew dark. The seat beside me vacant, I glanced across the aisle and up and down; everyone was asleep, necks lolling. Seemingly out of nowhere, Father Wright appeared, sliding into the seat next to me. The engine hummed rhythmically. I felt myself surrendering to exhaustion. And then something roused me, a strange discomfort. Father Wright had his hand down my trousers.

Utter shock. I began to exclaim, but he put his hand over my mouth.

We made a pit-stop in Canberra. When we got back on the bus, one of the Torres Strait Islander women who my parents knew, insisted she was sitting next to me all the way to Melbourne. She was strangely adamant. Had she seen something?

When we finally arrived, I first spent some time billeted with a family in Malvern, alone. Then we all came to the big presbytery in Werribee where we stayed for the rest of our time in Melbourne. Our delegation included hundreds of Aboriginals. One night there was a huge corroboree and bonfire, where Elders from the Cape danced by the flames. I stood by myself, watching the spectacle. I noticed Father Mick Peters, who I liked a lot, standing at a distance by himself, also. I thought about joining him, but it was so dark and disorientating.

And that's when Father Wright came up behind me, startling me once again. Who knew the man could move with such stealth? He grabbed my arms and pulled me in to him, rubbing himself against me. I felt his erect penis in my lower back. After a few moments I managed to wriggle free. Wading through the dark, I reached Father Peters; and for the rest of the night stayed at his side. I was scared and I feeling so alone, too ashamed to tell anyone and not really knowing how to, anyway. On the journey back to Queensland, I made sure I sat next to Margaret or the Torres Strait Islander woman, who persisted in not letting me out of her sight.

For the next few years I was careful to avoid being near Father Wright, despite his constant presence in the Aboriginal rights' movement. I didn't ever tell anyone what he did: the shame was too great, and I know my mother would have stopped me going out. That would have been worse, as it was my only escape from her scrutiny. Ironically, she felt I couldn't get up to any trouble at Catholic events. And in time, unfortunately because I never told anyone, I managed to suppress the memory enough to let my guard down.

***

As a teenager from a strict Catholic family attending a convent boarding school, my romantic fantasies attached themselves to the closest males—the priests in my orbit. Every year at school we used to go on a spiritual retreat down the beach with the priests. The nuns never came, just the priests and no one else—just us girls. At these retreats, I tried to stand out somehow, get the priests' attention and spend time alone with them. I never *did* anything, but looking back, I detect a pattern of attention-seeking. Sometimes I refused to participate in activities or discussions so that the priests were compelled to take me aside and ask if I was okay. At other times I would harness my creativity and shine to make sure they saw me.

Frequently, we girls, 15 and 16-year-olds, headed down to St Peters presbytery to socialise with the priests. They would bring out the wine, rum and scotch and we'd all drink. I had a huge crush on Father Patrick; a sweet man in charge of marriage coun-selling and administration at the diocese. As the alcohol flowed at the presbytery, I told him about my miserable home life; how mum and George were always fighting when I visited on the weekends, how they were both grumpy with me, how I had to look after my sisters as well as study, how I was playing guitar with my brother around town for pocket money. I also confided in him that I had started taking my mother's pills, Serepax and Valium. I wanted to tell him about other, darker things too, but I couldn't find the words or the opening. Mum knew I was taking some of her pills, but she knew nothing about her teenage daughter getting drunk with the priests.

Like everything else in the restless 70s, the Church was changing. When the charismatic movement came to Rocky, all us musical types flocked to church. We played instruments, swayed and clapped, sang 'Hail to God'. At school, some younger nuns joined the teaching staff, who, inspired by Vatican II, were more modern and liberal. They didn't wear a habit and were kind and welcoming. Some lay teachers arrived as well—women who came to school wearing regular dresses!

In Year 11 at the ripe age of 16 years, the nuns thought we could manage sex education the Catholic way. We got marched down to the local boys' school for classes. Of course, the nuns, priests and brothers would talk about anything *but* sex. Marriage, virginity, celibacy—these were all fine, but in the meantime, all my friends were smoking grass and sleeping with the neighbourhood boys.

At one sex ed session, the nuns and priests convened a panel of local Catholic parents to come in and tell us about their version of love, marriage and intimacy. A well-known local solicitor, Paul Brady, was on the panel with his wife, Frances, describing how love 'changes over time' but that in a Catholic marriage, couples stay together regardless. I had no idea what they meant, so I boldly asked a question.

'But isn't love, love?' I interrogated them. 'How *can* it change over time?'

They responded with a homily about how marriages go through different stages, children come along, people get older, companionship becomes more important than... They trailed off. Baffled, I quickly tuned out.

About 20 years later, I was running an Aboriginal women's business workshop for white women when an attractive lady in bohemian dress approached me.

'Hello, Pam,' she smiled. 'Do you remember me? I'm Frances Brady.'

'Oh, hello, Mrs Brady. How are you?' I said.

'I'm very well,' she grinned. 'But I'm not Mrs Brady anymore!'

The end of high school loomed. My marks were underwhelming as far as my mother was concerned. While I was aware that teachers expected less from an Aboriginal girl than they did from the other students, my mother would have none of that. Education was all, she believed. We all had to go to university, and that was that—this at a time when the proportion of students in Australia finishing Year 12 let alone going on to university was tiny. Mum was very forward thinking at that time. She didn't finish Grade 3 herself, and she was angry about that. She always felt that if she had had an education, things could have been different for her. She didn't want us to be cleaners or labourers, she said. She was determined that we would get out of the cycle of poverty and, for some reason, she thought it would help us deal with racism and its consequence of being treated as second-class citizens. The major crises at home arose when James declared that he wanted to be an electrician, and Su Anne wanted to be a ballerina—she'd been on point shoes since she was a child and had studied at a prestigious ballet school.

'You're going to university, anyway,' mum growled at her.

But at this time, I didn't give a stuff about my middling marks. I was taking too many of her pills and drinking with the priests at the cathedral after guitar practice. I was also spending my time singing around town rather than staying in with the books.

I was considering going to Woden Valley Hospital in Canberra, or some other hospital, to train as a nurse, because that did not require a university degree. And I had the experience of those summers working as a nursing aide at the local hospital, looking after babies the first year, in the men's ward the next. But in the end, I got into teachers' college in Rockhampton—it was the only course I got into—and mum insisted I stay home and do that.

Then another idea took root in my mind, and I told mum that I really wanted to stay with some of the old ladies up in the Cape. I was referring to some of our matriarchal Elders at Cape York. Not for the first time I was telling her I wanted to learn the business, but this time she was more open to the idea.

'Finish your first year of uni and then we can talk about it,' she said.

With the end of high school, my friendship group gradually splintered. Heidi, who lived in the Fijian resort, had moved to Europe years earlier after her father shifted the family to Switzerland. My Chinese friend went to uni and became a doctor. Jeannie lost touch for a while. Carmel got married, then divorced and left town. And incidentally, Sister Jean-Marie, the cruel nun who welcomed the Marilyn Monroe look-alike into her room every night, left the school and the Sisters of Mercy, to start a relationship with another woman.

6

THE 'BLACK END'

In early adulthood I spent a great deal of energy defying and out-manoeuvring mum and her expectations around my success and moral virtue. I felt this amorphous anger and resentment towards her, unaware that in coming years the emotional and physical distance between mum and me would blanket me in grief.

Learning how to bide my time, I did what I was told for the first year after finishing high school, enrolling in a teaching course at Capricornia Institute of Advanced Education in Rocky while living at home, where the atmosphere turned increasingly sour. Doors slammed. George ranted. Mum knocked back the sedatives and grew even more remote. I thought, God, my family has metamorphosed from the pleasant cocoon it had been during my childhood into a boring soap opera. (Later, my parents separated for a brief period: George moved into a boarding house until my brother, Kevin, came and got him; and eventually reconciled them.)

My only salvation was going to college, singing and hanging out with my friends. But for all this burgeoning independence, my social scene still revolved around the priests, just as it had through my teens. Frances' older sisters hung out with them, and because she and I used to sing at Mass together, we fell in with the crowd, drinking with them, playing guitar. The older girls flirted more confidently with the priests; we were self-conscious, but hopelessly infatuated. I was still stuck on Father Patrick. After I got my drivers' licence, he let me borrow his Holden Kingswood; I would go to the beach at night, or to Emu Park, a small fishing town north-east of Rocky, and loaf around. Patrick trusted me in a way my parents never did.

But I was bloody miserable and desperate to escape my family and Rockhampton. Teachers' college bored me crazy. While I enjoyed Child Psychology and learning how to foster children's creativity through art, all I really wanted to do was foster my own creativity, and sing. Still, I had to be realistic about my scheming, and take it one step at a time. Knowing my mother wouldn't let me leave Rocky on my own, I asked my fellow teaching student, Frances—a good Catholic girl and fellow graduate from The Range Convent—if she would consider moving with me to Brisbane where we'd finish our degree at McAuley College. She agreed. And, as I pointed out to mum, by moving to Brisbane I'd be near my sister, Patricia, who could keep a watchful eye on me.

The scheming paid off and then some: I collected Abstudy— federal government support for Aboriginal students—and the bishop at Rocky gave me a Catholic Education scholarship of $50 a fortnight. The priests also organised a house for us in Hill End, near West End, in Brisbane's inner south, just two streets away from the river and ferry. We shared with a man who belonged to the local West End Catholic Parish, so the rent was only $40 a fortnight.

Boarding the train to Brisbane, liberated from my mother and the seemingly endless household chores, I felt exhilarated beyond belief.

***

I was determined to seduce him. During my first year at teacher's college, Patrick and I found ourselves alone one night in the hallway at the presbytery. I'd worn my sexiest dress, a red jersey number with a cowl neck. I was getting ready to go home; we were both drunk. Patrick leaned in and kissed me. Properly. Everyone was trying to get priests to kiss them, so this was a victory of sorts. Enough of a victory for me, at this point; I thought about what mum might say, and rushed home, flustered.

But someone else was a fixture on the scene, worming his way back into my life. Father Leo Wright ran St Martin's Aboriginal Hostel in Brisbane for the Catholic Family Welfare Bureau, the hostel catering for young Aboriginal men—most of them from the Cherbourg mission—doing apprenticeships in the city. Father Wright was attentive, playful and charming; and he made me feel the centre of attention. So, despite the memory of him molesting me as a child—a memory I managed to suppress most of the time—I was a young woman with rampaging hormones. The idea that someone wanted to have sex with me was, sickly, flattering.

On the evening of the picnic barbecue at St Martin's, I wore a summer dress with shoe-string straps. It was a pleasant gathering of hostel and church workers and assorted Catholic hangers-on, everyone relaxed, chatting and drinking. As the crowd thinned, Father Wright, clad in his priestly uniform, offered me a lift home in his beige Ford Falcon. We climbed on to the bench seats, and as he turned the corners I slid towards him slightly. When we arrived home I asked if he wanted a cold drink. His eyes darted round the kitchen.

'Is Frances home?' he asked.

'No,' I said. 'She's out.'

After he'd finished his drink, I walked him down the hallway to the front door; the bedroom was just off to the side. He stopped and turned back, moving in to kiss me on the cheek. Then he grabbed at me and I found myself manoeuvred into the bedroom, eased onto the bed, where he started kissing me all over and rubbing himself against me. Then he tried stuffing his penis into my vagina, panting from the effort, but I sensed he was limp.

'Go away,' I pleaded, scared, knowing what he might do to me.

He stopped. Springing up from the bed, he pulled his trousers back on, then walked out the door, cool and calm as always—a man of few words and haughty demeanour.

A girly voice in my head nagged, 'Well you finally got what you wanted'. And then a wave of nausea hit me, laced with a hurt and disgust that festered for many years before it burst into outrage, commanding all my attention.

From that day on, I did my best to avoid him just as I had three years earlier after the trip to Melbourne for the Eucharist Congress. I still saw him every Sunday when Frances and I turned up obediently for church. Watching him play the pious man, knowing the abuse he perpetrated in private, this man's hypocrisy began sowing in me the seeds of religious doubt. But still, I went to church, assuming that to do otherwise was a mortal sin. That's how brainwashed so many of us were.

Other than our church attendance on Sunday, Frances and I led disparate lifestyles. On weekends she caught the ferry to the University of Queensland's St Lucia Library and studied, whereas I spent most of the weekend in bed nursing a hangover after a hard night's partying on Friday. By Sunday afternoon I was ready for the beach. Sometimes I wandered down to the riverbank where I sat watching the traffic on the water, calm settling in.

And then, halfway through teachers' college, I fell in love.

Peter was also attending teachers' college. Blonde and athletic-looking, the girls all swooned over him. We'd been part of this big friendship group that used to hang around together—for about three months we circled one another, and then he asked me out to dinner. He thought I was fabulous; I thought he was terribly romantic. As it happened, I took heed of my mother's advice to be selective about boyfriends, and never divorce sex from love. With Peter on the scene I figured: it's time. The son of a publican, Peter hailed from a pretty wealthy background. His parents lived in Surfers Paradise, and he roomed with his grandmother in her stately home in the old-money Brisbane suburb of Ascot. We hung out at the beach, surfed, spent our nights dancing and drinking. He worked at the Hamilton Hotel, owned by a friend of his father's, so he liked to think of himself as flush with funds.

'You must meet my parents,' he said, one day, so we drove to Surfers for the big introduction. Peter's family home was a double-storey villa overlooking the Tweed River. Only his mother and sister were home; both of them polite, blonde and very white. As for Peter's father, we arranged to meet him for lunch at his pub at Kirra Beach.

Peter and I arrived there before the lunchtime rush and grabbed a table in the bistro. His father, a tall man in late middle age, his hair as light as the rest of the family's, walked into the room and locked his eyes on us. On me. As Peter scrambled to his feet, his father swivelled on his heels and walked back out. Peter looked at me, alarmed. He rushed out the door to his father.

He was gone for about 20 minutes. I sipped my drink, wondering what was going on. When Peter returned he seemed pale and agitated.

'What's going on?' I asked him.

'Dad didn't know you were Aboriginal.'

Later that day, Peter's mother confided in me that she thought it unlikely her husband would ever soften his stance. Some months later, Peter told me his father threatened to cut off

51

all financial help unless he dumped me. He was distraught, flabbergasted. He said his parents had never said a bad word about Aboriginals, had never displayed any racism or taught him and his sister to regard Aboriginal people as inferior or different.

'I never knew he was racist,' Peter said.

After struggling for a few months, knowing I couldn't marry into a family that didn't' want me because of my skin colour, I felt our relationship was doomed before it even began.

After one semester of teachers' college in Brisbane, I quietly dropped out and looked for work, landing a job with the University of Queensland medical hearing team. As the team made annual visits to the Cape York communities to test the hearing of Aboriginal kids, the position also offered an ideal opportunity to fulfil my longstanding wish to bond with some clan Elders and absorb more of the knowledge. So, I signed on for the field trip with the understanding I'd be recording audiology on people's ears and logging the data. What I did not fully understand was that this trip would also mark my first confronting encounter with remote Aboriginal Australia.

At Kowanyama, a town on the Gulf of Carpentaria side of Cape York Peninsula, the people were scrawny-looking with gingery hair. The white manager of the Aboriginal mission lorded over his subjects in dictatorial fashion; everyone needed his permission not only to leave the town, but even to return. He wore military-style khaki clothing and carried a riding crop that he flicked against his thigh. Local Aboriginals lived in government housing, shopped at the one well-stocked store and drifted in and out of the offices of a small army of specially deployed bureaucrats: nurses, social workers, welfare officers, teachers.

At Mitchell River, I watched the old ladies cast out enormous lines into the water, reeling in enormous barramundi that would be flapping at the ends. The bilingual school was well-resourced and orderly in appearance; when years later, under the new policy of self-determination, the Aboriginals took over the town's governing, those same schools crumbled with neglect. At night, every night, the townspeople swarmed to the canteen and drank themselves into oblivion. Every night I lay awake listening to a chaotic symphony of moaning, screaming and shattering glass.

Further south at Edward River, we stayed at a place abutting a crocodile farm. Each morning I stepped out the front door to be greeted by the sight of them. It reminded me of when one of my uncles, a thorough-going crocodile hunter, turned up at our house with stuffed crocs—one of his souvenir skins was displayed on our wall. Some mornings we went out mud-crabbing before getting to work, and in the evenings, we feasted on shrimps from the river.

My time on Palm Island proved yet more illuminating, and more traumatic. The island is breathtakingly beautiful, an undulating landscape of tropical rainforest and rugged mountain ranges. But this was 1976 and the island's ugly history bled into the present. In the late 1800s, Chief Protector J.W. Bleakley designated Palm Island as 'a penitentiary for troublesome cases', a function that persisted through much of the 20th century when the Queensland government forcibly resettled Aboriginals there who were deemed 'disruptive', such as women pregnant from white men.

From our base we caught views of Fantome Island in the Coral Sea, an eerie dumping ground, first, in the 1920s, for Aboriginals afflicted by venereal disease, and a decade later, for lepers. When the leprosarium closed in 1973 it was purged by fire, the island condemned to a vast burial ground.

I confronted the first of several rude shocks when I tried organising my own living arrangements, blissfully ignorant of the segregation in force on the island. The hearing team was accommodated at the 'white end', the unofficial border marked by Mango Avenue, which Aboriginals had built. The border had once been explicit with gates at both ends of the road barring entry to non-whites—by the 1970s the geographic apartheid was more subtle. I wanted to stay with my Aunty Beryl, a senior clan relative, who naturally resided at the 'black end'. But the mission manager—a typically oppressive bureaucrat who threw children into the watchhouse to sleep on dirty mattresses for the most minor infringements—had the power to decide. And he decided I would sleep at the white end.

I looked out in the direction of Aunty Beryl's place and imagined myself leaping over a small hill and walking straight across the island to the black end. Yet the view was deceptive, it concealed the vast distances, the peaks and troughs. I soon discovered that getting to 'the other side', down to the ocean and back again was an epic journey that took all day.

One afternoon the hearing team organised a bush walk; among the walkers was some staff from the local primary school, a teacher and a building worker. The teacher invited us over for a party that evening. I drank, a bit too much. Feeling drowsy I wandered into a bedroom for a lie down. A short time later I woke to find this white guy on top of me—the building worker from the school. I pushed him off and rushed home.

The next day I rationalised the incident as just one of those things that happened on the notoriously dangerous Palm Island where shocking cruelty was almost a matter of routine. I was not going to create a ruckus in this community. What would be the point? The police wouldn't believe me, and I think it occurred to a lot to Aboriginal girls on the Island. It would just be a heartache to try.

My Aunty Beryl was a diminutive bespectacled woman. Like most blacks on the island she lived in an overcrowded house, but she maintained it lovingly and it had a gorgeous verandah shaded by a big mango tree. I visited her regularly during my stay. She taught me law, told me stories. Sometimes we just sat together in peaceful silence on the verandah. When the white mob from the mission office saw me with her, they ordered me back to the white section. I rolled my eyes at Aunty Beryl; she smiled and nodded at me to go. This happened almost every day after work before dinner—they knew I'd be there so they made a daily occurrence of it.

Despite this, she was able to pass on stories that connected me with my heritage. One of these, the story about the green ant and the golden spider, actually helped shaped my politics.

'In the dreaming, the animals were gigantic,' she began.

Between the trees and the shrubs lived an enormous golden spider that spun an expansive golden web. Meanwhile below the gum trees, thrived a community of shimmering green ants that left a trail of white slime and clumps behind them. As time went on, the spider and the ants began getting in each other's way; the spider spun his web over the ant trails, the ants wrecked the web. The other animals in the bush were getting sick of the conflict as it was a threat to *kanyini*, harmony on the planet. So the animals asked *Biaime*—God, the creator—to come down and mediate the conflict. So *Biaime* gathered the ants' little white clumps and buried them in the earth.

'That's called asbestos,' he said.

Next, he gathered the golden webs and buried them too.

'And that's called uranium.'

Biaime commanded the animals: 'You must never, never dig either of these up—if you do, you'll release vanity and ego into the world.'

There's a similar story about the Ranger Uranium Mine in the Northern Territory. It is said the rainbow snake, *Didjbi didjb*i, lives in the tailings dam at the bottom of the mountain range and that if the snake is disturbed it will signal the destruction of the earth. The Aboriginals over there get very nervous if the tailings dam starts leaking; they even disclosed this legend to the mining company to ensure they take care not to awaken the rainbow serpent.

I'm occasionally conflicted about this hardline anti-uranium message: what about uranium for nuclear energy—wouldn't this serve the greater good? I guess the answer is to tap solar energy or other renewable sources.

Aunty also instructed me in the three laws of respect: for yourself, for others and for *Ngura*, the land.

'Your great-grandfather taught the young men in our clan the same laws,' she said. 'Respecting yourself is the most important, that's why it comes first. You must never put other people before yourself.' Maybe she saw that something inside me was damaged.

When I returned home from the Cape I confided in my mother about the incident with the building worker at the party. She grimaced.

'You're a silly girl for getting drunk.'

***

But I was done with moral judgments and being dictated to. Back in Rocky, my head a riot of thoughts after wandering on the Cape, I arrived at a grim resolve. I wrote Peter a letter telling him we were through, that I did not want to marry him. I told him I had met someone else—a lie, of course. Though I was melancholy about ending the relationship, I knew our options were few. His father was never going to accept me. (In the years that followed I occasionally found myself nostalgic about our time together—at random moments, I called him up, murmuring down the line, 'I miss you'.)

And I dropped out of teachers' college.

'I'm not coming back,' I told Frances. 'You can rent out my room'.

At that point my mother stopped talking to me. A silence that lasted years.

I caught a train to Brisbane, moved into an apartment with another friend, resumed working at the University of Queensland—and quit that job, too, before the year was out. As Christmas approached, I packed a small bag of clothes, vacated the apartment and made my way to the interstate freeway. I was 19. The road shimmered in the heat. I put my thumb out for the southbound traffic.

A truck slowed down.

7

ON THE ROAD

I hitched to Melbourne, Adelaide, Brisbane and back again to Melbourne. As soon as I arrived at one place, I hitched a ride somewhere else; it didn't even matter that I was frequently travelling backwards rather than forwards. As long as I was moving, I was happy.

A psychologist might say I was in a dissociative fugue.

At one of the truck stops, I struck up a conversation with a guy called Ken, an employee of one of the trucking companies, a thick, muscle-bound man with handle-bar moustache and tattoos, clad in regulation King Gees. He seemed a cheerful sort. I climbed in the back of his 22-wheeler alongside his kelpie, the other stray dog.

Ken taught me how to drive the truck, and soon enough I was expert at it. He taught me how to change tyres. We delivered watermelons to the Melbourne market. We drove to Adelaide, taking turns driving and sleeping, country and Western music playing on the cassette deck. I took showers at the truckies' lounge and wolfed down burgers and Coke.

'Fuck me,' I thought, 'this is freedom'.

Ken asked few questions and covered all my expenses, occasionally slipping me 50 or 100 bucks. A married man with kids, he never tried to take advantage of me.

By about March the following year we arrived in Perth, Ken's hometown. Now, inexplicably, I decided I'd had enough trucking. Ken had some mates who were staying in a caravan park, so I hung out with them, bidding him goodbye. As we say these days, my decisions were totally random.

I knew I had to find work fast. I saw a job advertisement seeking someone with experience in earth-moving equipment for a project in the town of Beverley, east of Perth. Uncertain about the chances of a girl scoring such a job, I decided to give it a whirl, anyway.

'You ever graded a road?' asked the guy on the phone.

'Nah, but I've driven trucks.'

'Alright, then.'

So I got on a bus to Beverley, a small wheatbelt town on the Avon River. For a few days I stayed in the pub, then the boss found me a place to live. On the job, I learned how to drive a grader, carve out contour banks for farmers, dig dams with the bulldozer. After about three months I grew weary and needed medical treatment for a minor accident, so I returned to the caravan park in Perth. Feeling somewhat lost, I wandered into the local branch of the Commonwealth Employment Service, as it was then known, and told them my story.

The bloke behind the desk said: 'We're looking for some Aboriginal people with a bit of smarts for a job in Canberra'.

Never having been to the national capital before, I liked the sound of that.

My airline ticket was booked. On the morning of the flight a Commonwealth driver in a white uniform turned up at the caravan park in a Mercedes Benz to take me to the airport—those were the good old days of public service largesse!

With the Commonwealth's formal entry into Aboriginal affairs in the early 1970s, there was a push to employ more Aboriginal people in the public sector. When I arrived in Canberra, in September 1978, the Department of Social Security had established an Aboriginal services unit, the first of its kind, and was running an employment training scheme for Indigenous people. They taught me about this thing called binary codes, which I found fascinating.

The Department then flew me 'home' to Perth to work for a month in their office in St George's Terrace. There, in a sterilised habitat—no cords, no dust—encased in a gigantic six-foot glass box, lived their first PC computer. We loaded big tapes into the machine and read codes. We wore white coats. The computer clanked along.

At the Department of Finance in the basement of the Treasury Building in Canberra where I did my practical computer operator training, they had a massive, rumbling IBM computer that printed out Social Security welfare cheques and Annual Group Certificates. I loved doing this, at first. I thought it was pretty clever. I had no idea that computers would be such a huge change for the world, but for me it was an exciting and interesting time.

After my 12 months' training, I successfully negotiated with the Department to stay in Canberra. I liked it there. After moving out of the public servants' accommodation at Macquarie House in Barton, I lived in the suburb of Red Hill in a house with serene grounds, and worked in the ghostly Juiliana House in Woden. Landing a job in the Department of Finance, I settled into a lifestyle of working hard and partying even harder. After work, a bunch of Aboriginal bureaucrats would head to what we called 'The Soul', a bar in the basement of the large MLC building in Woden where they all worked, and where the neo-classical statue of a nude lady in the front window welcomed the thirsty patrons.

At The Soul I started drinking heavily for the first time, guzzling scotch and tequila, polishing off a bottle at a time. And then everyone would drive home drunk! In a stupor, I would spin round the concentric roads on Capital Hill, round the first circle and further down to State Circle and Parliament Drive. 'Err...' I wondered vaguely, 'where's the road?'

The night usually ended with me falling into bed with some guy, the mood casual, lackadaisical.

On one such night I fell into bed with Fitz, who I met through a mutual friend. A cameraman at the local TV station, Fitz was a wiry and energetic type with a moustache. Did it occur to me he had the same name as my white ancestor, the 19th-century pastoralist? The two of us were enjoying a more or less exclusive relationship when I got pregnant by accident.

The timing was lousy. I lived in temporary public service accommodation, with no family, no roots in Canberra. My mind flitted through various scenarios. Maybe I could go to Cairns? Find a job up north, settle somewhere far away from my mother, whose absence remained a source of relief as well as pain? But the head of the Aboriginal unit, a woman, pleaded with me to have an abortion.

'If you have a baby at your age, it'll ruin your life and career,' she said. 'Trust me—I'm talking from experience. You should be going back to uni, not having a baby.'

I gave in; she helped organise a visit to the abortion clinic in Sydney. It was the sensible thing to do even if part of me was crying out in grief, remembering how sweet my siblings were when they were little, overwhelmed by my primal love for babies.

With the news of my pregnancy, Fitz began to withdraw, and even after my abortion, for which he had eagerly advocated, he was non-committal. In the aftermath of the abortion I was a miserable, hormonal mess.

We were watching a band at the ANU bar one night when, wanting to wipe myself out, I washed down some Serepax with a bottle of scotch. As soon as we got back to Fitz's place, I passed out. He called the doctor. For about four days I drifted in and out of sleep.

Fitz and I were ending. I was unravelling.

Cut to another scene with some friends at the Canberra food and wine festival, where I drank some more—a lot more. I remember thinking, 'I'm a piece of shit'. I stumbled out of the restaurant, and approached Commonwealth Avenue, a four-lane highway; Lake Burley Griffin, still and glassy in the near distance. I planted myself in the middle of the freeway. Flung my arms wide. Waited for a car to mow me down.

The sound of tyres screeching to a halt. Someone grabbed me by the arm.

'What the hell are you doing?' It was a male voice.

At the hospital I watched this man whisper something to a woman on duty. The woman approached me.

'I'm a social worker.' Her voice was kind.

'I had an abortion,' I moaned. 'Then my boyfriend left me.'

And I told the social worker about Father Leo Wright, about how he had abused me. About how I felt so hopeless, I could no longer sing or play the guitar. About my mother, how I wanted to tell her about the abortion, how I did not want to tell her about the abortion, how she never gave me any attention, how I longed for her.

'I want you to come and see me every few weeks,' the social worker said. 'Now go home and get some sleep.'

Some weeks later I moved in with the already legendary John Newfong, the first Aboriginal person to be employed by the mainstream print media. At the time I met John, he was changing from full-time journalist—having worked at the *Sydney Morning Herald*, *The Australian* and *The Bulletin*— to firebrand political activist. Six years earlier he had been the 'chief spokesperson' for the Aboriginal Tent Embassy, an iconic land rights protest on the lawns of Old Parliament House; he'd coined the memorable phrase, 'the mission has come to town'. Now he edited the Indigenous magazine, *Identity*. He was also gay. I met him regularly at the gay bar in town when I was out drinking and dancing. We struck up a friendship; he invited me to rent a room at his townhouse. He fast became my close friend and protector, dragging me out at night, forcing me onto the dancefloor. He commissioned me to write an article for the new *Identity* mag about glaucoma and trachoma in remote Aboriginal communities.

And on the night I locked myself in my room, sobbing into the pillow, I heard a tentative knock on my door.

'Are you okay?' John asked.

The story of my climb out of depression is quirky and counter-intuitive. It centres on another towering icon of Aboriginal liberation, Charlie Perkins, soccer star, the first Aboriginal university graduate, veteran of the 1965 Freedom Rides. For most of 1979, I had been going to these barbecues that Charlie held once a month at his place in the Canberra suburb of Pearce. People would talk jobs and politics, scheming over sausage and beer.

Towards the spring of that year, Charlie, a married man in his 40s and a powerful figure in the Department of Aboriginal Affairs, said to me: 'I'd like to come round to your place for a visit'. 'Righto,' I replied, naive as ever.

On the designated date, I was baking a cake for the occasion. A friend of mine was around, and I told her that Charlie would be popping round for a chat. She laughed.

'Don't be stupid. He wants to have a thing with you!'

'You reckon?'

So she stayed with me at the house, and Charlie never came. When I saw him again a short time later, he explained that he'd come around that day but left when he heard voices in the house. I thought, yeah, he is interested after all. And as often happens in such circumstances, the flattery proved powerful and I started getting interested in him.

Charlie was also on the board of Aboriginal Hostels Limited, and they were having a convention at a fancy hotel in Sydney, the one beneath the Coca Cola sign. Charlie organised for me to travel to Sydney, too, at the Commonwealth's expense. I was put up at another hotel across the road from the fancy one. Coincidentally, Father Patrick was also in Sydney for a Catholic conference. I had kept in touch with him, intermittently, partly because of my lingering crush on him, partly because I was hoping he might relay some information about me to my mother. At least she'd know where I was and that I was doing okay.

So, I caught up with him: we went for a ferry ride and ate dinner at the Cross.

'What's going on?' Patrick eventually asked. 'What exactly are you doing here?'

'I'm having an affair with Charlie Perkins.' I wasn't really, just contemplating the possibility at the time, which was why I was in Sydney. But it was eventually to come about.

He was horrified, telling me, 'I'm really angry with Charlie about this, he shouldn't do this!'

But having sex with Charlie was weird—I felt like I was his daughter, being just a few years older than his eldest. I was 20 and he would have been at least 45. After only one encounter I told him: 'I don't think we should be doing this'.

From that day on Charlie and I became lifelong friends. And for reasons I cannot entirely explain I felt suddenly lighter, sensed the cloud had lifted from over me. When some weeks later I got dolled up for the launch of the latest edition of *Identity* at the National Press Club, an edition that included a story of mine, my mood was conspicuously sunny.

8

PRESS GALLERY

A tab was going at the bar, the mood buzzing at the Press Club. Already feeling tipsy, I got talking to a woman called Kay who worked in the office of Jim Keefe, a Queensland Labor senator known to my parents.

'Have you met my brother?' Kay said.

I cast my eyes over a man in his late 30s. A mass of curly black hair. Cameras dangled from his neck, a kitbag with yet more cameras was strapped across his shoulder. He was wearing a loud, oriental-style shirt with a tall collar and thick pink-and-white stripes and, despite the heat, a leather coat that almost brushed the floor, a coat that I would soon learn was his signature garment. A glass of scotch in his hand. A smile on his face. Late that night, 'I feel like I've known you forever'. Thus spoke William Errington: freelance photojournalist, renowned war correspondent and my future husband.

We talked, about everything. We drank, a lot. I knocked a bottle of wine over the red and white chequered tablecloth. I felt mortified, but William just laughed and ordered a new one. As the night wore on, the room took flight and so did I. Climbing onto the table, I stood up and shot a finger into the air. 'You're all racists!' I shrieked, at no one in particular, swaying like a madwoman. At that point William bundled me up and took me back to his place where I crashed on his sofa while he slept in his bedroom.

And for the next few months, William courted me diligently. He took me to the movies, to dinner, to functions at the National Press Club. He bought me flowers and gifts. As a woman barely out of my teens, being courted by an older man felt very romantic. And for an often, fearful young woman, William's fearlessness was exhilarating. He shared a house with another journalist and played snooker at the Press Club with the biggest names in the trade. He took unflattering photographs of Prime Minister Malcolm Fraser for the newspaper; whenever Fraser saw William he'd make a snide remark about the images. In the previous decade, the 1970s, he took black and white shots of the police tearing down the Aboriginal Tent Embassy on the lawn of Parliament House. He snapped Charlie Perkins obeying police orders and removing a peg in the tent. Charlie was probably trying to mediate a resolution to the protest, but in those militant times the photograph carried a negative connotation.

It was William who gave me permission to stop attending Mass on Sunday. I was still turning up at this cathedral down the road, even though I had been wavering in my Catholicism for some time, as I became more aware of the church's hypocrisy, including its own sorry history in eroding Aboriginal culture. At the same time, I weighed all this against the Church's generous investment in Aboriginal welfare. I remembered my activist days in the Rockhampton housing association. I remembered the local bishop who worked with mum, supporting her efforts as a community organiser, handing out scholarships to kids who wanted to pursue study. Look, the Church *was* patronising. We were their lost cause, their fallen flock. But it's also true that its heart was now in the right place. Wasn't it?

One Sunday, William said, 'You don't *have* to keep going to Mass, you know'.

'But I've been told it's a mortal sin, if I don't.'

'Really?'

So, I stopped going: lo' and behold nothing happened to me.

One of eight siblings, William came from a Scottish-Irish family of soldiers and sailors. His father, a navy veteran, was a refrigeration engineer who they said modified the humidicrib to the modern version. The family had several boats moored near their home at Pittwater, the gorgeous waterway separating the New South Wales Central Coast from greater Sydney. Two of William's three brothers served in the Vietnam War, and he too, had served there as a press photographer, an experience that forced him to count his blessings and live joyfully. He once told me, 'Every day I wake up and think, thank God I'm not in a wheelchair'.

But Vietnam cast a shadow over William, a shadow longer than even he realised. He had been married before the war. He said that on his return to Australia his wife absconded with their children, a daughter aged 13 and a son aged two. His efforts to trace them came to nothing; his grief became a permanent wound. He did not see his daughter again until she was grown up, with children of her own, and had contacted him at *The Canberra Times*. While I admittedly only know his side of the story, it always struck me that his ex-wife had been terribly cruel.

William's parents and siblings welcomed me with open arms, though on one occasion his mother, Joan, made a curious confession. 'If it was one of my daughters going out with an Aboriginal man I'd be concerned because I wouldn't think an Aboriginal man would be able to take care of my daughters.' I remembered my mother's damning assessment of black men: 'No point marrying a black man'.

'But I'm not concerned about you,' Joan continued. 'My son will look after you; I'm sure you'll be a wonderful mother.' That such sentiments might be construed as racist simply never occurred to me.

Six months after that drunken night at the Press Club I moved in with William. As Christmas of that same year, 1979, drew near he urged me to send mum a card.

'Just to let her know you're alive,' he said.

And so I did.

Long-term commitment was the last thing on my mind, however. I began hearing George's voice in my head, urging me to: 'Go and become a doctor'. In the new year, I decided to heed that call and try to enrol in Medicine. First, I brushed up on physics and chemistry for a semester, at Narrabundah College. In second semester, I studied at night school at Dickson College where I continued the crash course for entry, all the while supporting myself with a job in Admin at the Department of Defence.

A journalist friend of William's, another William—Bill D'arcy, lived in an enormous house in Deakin from where he broadcast a program that aired on 3AW. D'arcy was good mates with Bob Hawke, then the president of the ACTU and being primed for a seat in federal parliament. Bob told D'arcy he was going to buy one of the new, swish apartments that were being built on Telopea Park in Kingston, an attractive suburb in Canberra. He said he wanted to rent it out for a while and asked D'arcy if he knew anyone who'd be interested in the offer. William stuck his hand up, as we lived across Telopea Park in Barton.

We moved to the unit in early 1980. We bought a fancy double bed and a friend lent us some other furniture; William stuck his three marijuana plants[2] outside the front door. It was at this time, too, that he bought me a piano for my 21st birthday, praising my musical talent.

---

2   It was legal at that time in the ACT only, for an individual to own a maximum of 3 marijuana plants.

Part of the arrangement that Bob requested was that we always leave the sliding door unlocked so he could show guests the apartment whenever he wished. There was a downside to this arrangement, of course. The home's proximity to Parliament House made it a convenient hang-out for Press Gallery journos during the day, even when William was away covering some war or conflict overseas. His journo mates would congregate in our dining room at lunchtime, drinking and smoking dope. I found this ritual bloody annoying, especially because I had stopped drinking ever since the night I met William at the Press Club; and I'd never smoked dope because I was taught that people who smoked dope ended up heroin addicts. In fact, I was on a health kick, running around the lake, swimming, riding my bike, and experimenting with vegetarianism and yoga.

So, I routinely came home from my night job behind the bar at the Italian club to find the fridge emptied of food, a mass of dirty plates on the dining table and a halo of smoke above it. That's because as soon as word spread that something was up at Parliament the journos all rushed out the door, leaving me with the mess. I don't know why they didn't stay put though since they used to like saying, 'never let the facts fuck up a good story'. One of these good stories they told me was about the female secretaries who worked in various offices of Parliament House and kept little black books listing the MPs they'd had sex with. Apparently, they had an elaborate rating system with different names attracting different coloured stars: a red star for sex with a backbencher, a silver star for a cabinet minister, and a gold star for shagging the Prime Minister.

Some weeks later, while I was sitting in the non-members bar in Old Parliament House waiting for William, I gazed out the window and saw underneath the pergola in the courtyard, a group of secretaries, dressed seductively in tight dresses and stilettos, wine glasses in hand, small notebooks on the table in front of them, all grinning and laughing. I thought to myself: 'Shit, it's true!'

Unfortunately, at some point I decided if you can't beat 'em, join 'em. William had persuaded me that smoking marijuana would not in fact lead to heroin addiction, so I began indulging. I say it was unfortunate that I succumbed because it led to an episode so embarrassing I never lived it down. It happened one afternoon when I had indulged in some very potent dope and found myself freaking out with paranoia. To calm me down, William put me under the shower.

As usual, when I came out, all the journos were planted round the dining room, smoking grass. I walked unsteadily towards them, still in a haze. At that point, I vaguely registered Bob Hawke knocking on the glass door and walking in with his secretary turned political advisor, Jean Sinclair. I heard him yell out, 'Oh Bill, I've just come round to show Jeannie,' a pause as he absorbed the dining room scene, 'the joint'.

Later, Bill D'Arcy and another journo called William—Bill Pinwill—told me I had sat down at the dining table and gazed out the window, totally zoned-out. And that William had said to me, 'Look, Bob's here. Say hello to him'. And that Hawke had tried to make conversation with me, but I was so off my face, I said nothing.

As I said, the guys never let me forget the day the future prime minister tried to chat with me, but I was too stoned to respond.

At the end of that year, with Bob elected as the member for Wills, he told us he'd be shifting into the apartment. We arranged to move around the corner to a house behind the Press Club that our friends had just vacated.

On the day he and Hazel moved into the apartment, we were mopping up, helping sort through the hand-over. Workmen came and went. Furniture was delivered. Bob, dressed in King Gee shorts, balanced a chair on the dining table, wanting to tighten the screws, but the phone kept ringing for him. He was harassed and agitated.

Hazel asked me to help her stack the dishwasher. I made the mistake of loading the machine with concentrated liquid, and now it was spitting foam all over the floor. Seeing the mess through the doorway, Bob growled from the lounge room, 'You're an idiot Hazel'.

Sheepishly, I confessed that I was the one who had put concentrate into the dishwasher, and that it wasn't his wife's fault. But Hazel just shot back,

'Shut the fuck up, Bob!'

Gesturing to William, she said, 'Let's go outside for a smoke'. So the two of them sat outside and smoked a joint, leaving Bob to his moods.

Not three years later, on 8 February 1983, Bob took over from Bill Hayden as leader of the Labor Party. On the same day, by remarkable coincidence, Prime Minister Fraser called a snap election for March 5, unwittingly setting in train Labor's historic landslide.

***

I could obviously manage sobriety when it mattered, because I got into medicine at the University of New South Wales. I was only the second Aboriginal in the medical school, my admission based entirely on merit and not on any Indigenous quota. Still, shortly after I arrived at the university the dean of medicine summoned me to his office.

'You *will* finish this course, won't you?' he asked. 'Tell me you're not going to go walkabout?' I told him I'd let him know if I was ever going to.

I rented a flat in Randwick, socialised, considered myself single again. But to my surprise, William contacted me all the time, and visited all the time. He wasn't about to let me go.

In first-year medicine, we dissected cadavers—that was fine by me. In the second year we had to be present during surgery and practise putting scalpels in people. I kept fainting. I returned to the dean's office, and said, 'I'm going walkabout'.

Back in Canberra, I again moved in with William. He was living in Curtin with Bill Pinwilll, ABC defence correspondent and another press veteran from the war in Vietnam and Cambodia. Bill had newspapers strewn all over the living-room floor. Every day after he left for work, I scooped up the papers and tossed them in the bin, until eventually, William said to me, 'Could you please leave his papers on the floor? That's his filing system.'

Meanwhile my professional milieu was changing along with my living arrangements. After stints working at the Italian Club and the Commonwealth Club, I landed a job with the recently-established Aboriginal Development Commission, working in the area of economic development. Suddenly I was thrust into the thick of Aboriginal politics in the early 1980s, a heady time of protests and marches. Eventually I moved into the Secretariat, undertaking research and being responsible directly to the commissioners. I loved the job, but the woman in charge of the Secretariat had a set against me, almost hate at first sight. I reckon her dislike had something to do with my developed wardrobe: William showered cash on me; I spent it in designer boutiques in Manuka and on Italian-label shoes.

But I copped harassment from high-profile men, too, who weren't focused on my footwear. After work one day I waited for William in the non-members bar of the Old Parliament House— something I did on a regular basis. So, there I was sipping a scotch when I noticed Clyde Holding who was then the Labor Minister for Aboriginal Affairs, slide up and sit on the stool next to me, and order a drink. Obviously, I knew who he was as I worked in Aboriginal Affairs and he was our Minister, but I'd never spoken to him before. He slid closer and whispered as his hand found contact with my knee 'Would you like to come home with me?' I quickly turned my gaze around the bar to see if anyone had heard him, shocked as I was, and noticed William rambling through the side door. I waved at him urgently, rolling my eyes, and he came over immediately, understanding what had gone on; Clyde was a legendary letch.

'You wanna get married?' It was a question William lobbed at me every now and then, his delivery relaxed. I didn't respond.

'Okay—you wanna get married?' I asked him one day, and so our decision was sealed.

William was tasked with organising the celebrant and the paperwork; the rest was all mine, including the invitations. One of William's friends, a newspaper cartoonist, drew a sketch of the two of us on a bike together, life rafts from William's boat, *Monsoon*, around our necks and our two cats in the wheel. We used this drawing as the wedding invite, announcing the wedding would be held at William's brother's place at Towlers Bay on the western foreshore at Pittwater. The guests would catch the ferry over from Church Point and ascend three steep walking tracks in the Ku-ring-gai Chase National Park to arrive at the Bay. Mildly arduous, we realised, but we felt confident our loved ones would go the extra mile in our honour.

'Want your family to come?' William asked.

'My mother's dead,' I said, a remark I often made because that's how it felt to me.

But William tracked my mob down, and without my knowing, invited them to our wedding. My sisters were enlisted as flower girls, my little brother as the musician and my mother was a rapturous mother-of-the-bride. It had been five years since I'd last seen any of them.

When the day came, I wriggled into a low-cut, white-and-gold threaded jumpsuit with jodhpurs—very 1980s! William donned a caftan of raw silk. A thought pricked at me.

'Where's the celebrant?' I asked.

William looked up at me, eyelids heavy; a friend had given him a block of Turkish hash and a pipe as a gift. He was making good use of it.

'I didn't organise one,' he said, all Zen-like.

'Are you fucking joking?' I shrieked.

Immediately, I commandeered Jan, a friend of ours, put her in a blue-and-white caftan and declared, 'You're the celebrant. Just act like you know what you're doing.'

We exchanged vows. Another friend played the flute. Jan acted like she knew what she was doing. We married. I smoked a heap of dope.

'Well that's okay, love,' my mother beamed, downing yet another glass of champagne. 'It's your wedding day.'

At the end of it all we sailed our boat over Pittwater Harbour and into the metaphorical sunset.

We were living in another house in Barton, but my work situation hadn't changed. I was sick of being harassed by the woman in the Secretariat; Charlie Perkins—then chair of the Commission, and later to be the secretary of the Department of Aboriginal Affairs—wouldn't move her. I wouldn't move. It was a Mexican standoff.

A couple of months after the wedding I flew to Perth for a conference of the Commission's Secretariat. After a meeting we all gathered at a restaurant. Charlie was there, too. Later that evening he slipped the key to his hotel room into my hand. Never mind that we hadn't had sex since that one night in Sydney in 1978. To be fair, all the male Aboriginal activists, married or not, got about, putting the hard word on nearly every woman in their orbit. The only person who did not sleep around, apart from the much older men, was Patrick (Paddy) Dodson.

When no one was around, I placed the key back in his hand.

'Charlie—see this ring? I'm married.'

On my return to work in Canberra the following week, I discovered I'd been demoted to the housing development section. I stormed into the chairman's office, slamming the door shut behind me.

'Is this because I didn't sleep with you?' I barked at Charlie.

'Hmm.' He looked at me sheepishly.

'You can't do that. This is a workplace, blackfellas can't act like that!.'

'Alright' he grumbled. And I got my job back.

But while Charlie was done harassing me, the woman in the secretariat was not. I was getting fed up with the job.

'I want to go back to singing and dancing,' I said one day to William, on a whim.

'How are you going to do that?'

I'd heard about the Aboriginal and Islander Dance Theatre in Sydney, I explained and I'm going to go to jazz and dance classes for the next six months, so I can audition.

'Maybe we could move there for a while? Stay with your family at Towlers Bay?'

For the rest of that year, 1982, I trained for the audition, every day a rigorous schedule of jazz and classical ballet classes. Again, the hard work paid off. I was accepted into the dance theatre, and by Christmas we were living with William's brother and his girlfriend at Towlers Bay. Each morning I steered a putt-putt boat to my car at Church Point, then I drove for ages, navigating choking traffic, to the theatre at Glebe. Every day I returned home after dark, numb with exhaustion.

I was in a class that included Stephen Page, now the artistic director at Bangarra Dance Theatre; he was a mean disco dancer. We danced in every discipline, I studied opera, we learnt cultural history from the actor, playwright and Aboriginal activist, Bob Maza, father of the now equally famous actress, Rachel Maza, and Aboriginal historian-filmmaker, Lester Bostock. When the daily commute became too wearisome, I moved into the theatre's hostel, living alongside fellow students much younger than me. For the most part, my new roommates were gratingly immature.

Elders from Aurukun came down from far north Queensland to teach us, and we went up to Yirrkala, in Arnhem Land, to learn from the Elders. I met Graham Mooney, who became a life-long friend; and I got to know Dorothea Randall, creator of a new Aboriginal dance style which married traditional and contemporary forms, and the daughter of 'Uncle' Bob Randall whose 1970s song, 'Brown Skin Baby (They Took Me Away)', became an anthem for the stolen generations. When I met Uncle Bob, we formed a bond so close he culturally adopted me. In late middle-age the renowned author, teacher and creator of the landmark documentary, *Kanyini*, returned to his mother's ancestral land at Mutitjulu, at the eastern end of Uluru. About 25 years later, Mutitjulu and the Randalls, played a starring role in a political intrigue that saw my name all over the media, for all the wrong reasons.

The AIDT often took us away to remote Aboriginal communities to learn traditional dance from Elders and involve ourselves in community cultural life. I went on my first cultural camp with Elders from Aurukun, held in bushland on the Hawkesbury River. The women lay me down, painted my body and decorated me with feathers. We young women learnt to weave, while the men taught the male students how to make spears. This was the first ceremony I had ever been involved in and it was special and sacred. I remember watching those Aurukun men and women dancing and singing, teaching us the same, telling us what to do and we dared not do anything until we were told. It was my first foray into the deep meaning of the *Tjukurpa* and I was overtaken with a joy I'd never felt. I could feel the spirits everywhere.

During the corroboree at night, I felt as if I was in a trance, at one with my own heartbeat. Afterwards, we went for a walk with an Elder. When a flock of white birds flew overhead, he pointed at them and said, 'Can you see the ancestors travelling with the birds?' And I saw Mimi spirits, fairy-like with their spidery, elongated bodies, dancing on the mountain ridges.

Another Elder, a rainmaker, said to the group, 'I will teach you a song and one of you will have permission for this song'. Then he sang the song to us. All through the night the song echoed and pulsated through me. The next morning, I told the rainmaker, 'I can't get the song out of my mind'. I sang it back to him, word for word.

'Well then,' he smiled.

It was me. I had permission to carry on the sacred, cleansing song, the rain song that, depending on how you rendered it, could draw from the clouds a thunderstorm, a trickle or a shower. It was also, I was told, a healing song. At the age of 24 I was finally starting to know myself, to understand that water and medicine were in my *Tjukurpa*, my dreaming.

Which is probably why, a short time after the camp, after William and I made love, I knew I had conceived.

9

TO BE WILLING

While my pregnancy naturally spelled the end of my dancing career it also ignited the idea of a road trip, as if we'd been called to family and the wild. At Towlers Bay we detached our fold-out tent from the back of a camper and packed it, and ourselves, into the four-wheel drive. We drove up to Rockhampton, to commune with my family, those years of estrangement now a dim memory. We stayed for three or four months, camped by the Fitzroy River. It was a relaxed, joyous time.

During this period I visited the local hospital—an illuminating experience, in a bad way. My old school friend, Carmel, had just given birth there, and my cousin was just about to. I found Carmel first; she was in the front section of the hospital in a cheerful, light-filled maternity ward. When I asked the nurse about my cousin's whereabouts, she said, 'Downstairs, follow me'.

I assumed she meant that Gladys was in another ward, somewhere. But the nurse led me down to the back of the hospital and out through the gate. To the side, was a separate ward with bars across the windows.

'In here,' the nurse said.

And that's where she was, inside a dark prison-like complex; she, and the other Aboriginal women. After that visit I said to William: 'There's no way I'm having my baby in this town'.

When we tired of Rockhampton we continued north along the coast, stopping at Townsville. By now I was seven months' pregnant and beginning to feel anxious.

'I'd rather have my child back in Canberra,' I told William, so we promptly turned around and headed south.

On our return to the capital we stayed with some friends in Barton. As I approached the last few weeks of my pregnancy I shopped around for doctors, hospitals and birthing options. Now I could barely walk. So one night, William and I addressed my heaving stomach.

'Arika (we'd already decided on her name!), we've had enough,' we announced. 'You have to come out.'

Sure enough, the next morning, the labour pains started.

When I was installed in the labour ward at Canberra hospital, I heard my mother's voice in my head, warning me: 'Don't lie on the bed; the best way to give birth is to squat'.

Some hours later, the nurses and the doctor stood observing me. I was vertical, breathing hard.

'She won't lie down,' one of the nurses implored the doctor. 'She won't stick her legs up.'

'Give her a mirror and let her do what she wants,' the doctor said.

So, the nurses gave me a mirror and a tub of warm water. I perched at the edge of the bed. In the evening William turned up carrying his camera gear and a large basket full of roses.

'We stole them from the Senate rose garden,' he grinned, explaining that he and the two Bills had gone down there and plucked them while the senate guards weren't looking. He plopped the basket on the table and grasped my hand. I was screaming with pain, drenched in sweat, the baby's head crowning. The nurses chose this moment to ask if I'd mind if a group of trainee midwives came in to observe. Incapable of speech, I must have nodded. William looked on, visibly terrified at the spectacle, me shrieking, a row of young nurses in the corner, their faces stunned and horrified. For once, my husband was too overwhelmed to take photos.

But when the moment came, when Arika came, it was quiet and peaceful. The nurse placed her on my chest and I looked down at a beautiful, peaceful, three-pound baby with black hair. The doctor turned to William.

'Would you like to cut the cord?' he asked.

'No way!'

We moved to Yarralumla in Canberra's inner south. Arika refused to stay in the cot I had bought for her; she insisted on sleeping between us in the marital bed. When she was eight weeks old a friend called me. Was I interested in a job at the Commonwealth Schools Commission? This was very tempting as I didn't want to simply stay home all day with a baby. William and I agreed that he take a year off to be the primary caregiver.

So, I returned to the workforce and William brought Arika to the office for breastfeeding. By the time he arrived, I'd be leaking. Then he'd pick me up after work and I would feed her on the way home. Later on, we hired an Indian nanny to help out, and later still, we enrolled Arika at the Chinese-Australian preschool because I wanted her to learn languages early. It was the only one in Canberra and it was the choice between it or the French-Australian school which was fully booked. It was a lovely time, despite the blues that descended on me every so often. Despite the fact I had started drinking again.

We bought a house with a garden in the leafy suburb of Narrabundah. After we moved in, I remarked on the unkempt state of the trees, shrubs and grass around the dwelling, although I wasn't much of a gardener myself, unlike my parents who always had meticulously kept gardens. They grew all kinds of vegetables and herbs—I could barely grow lawn.

'We have to do lots of gardening here,' I said to William.

'Nah,' he replied. 'Leave it. I want to grow a jungle.'

It was the first, subtle sign that a shadow was falling over my husband, and that I was following him into the thicket. Post-traumatic stress symptoms began to emerge in him, and he changed. I didn't understand what he meant by wanting to have a jungle all around the house. It was much later when I went to the Vietnam Veterans Counselling Service that I realised it was because he was probably having flashbacks of Vietnam or feelings about that time. The jungle may have been a safe hiding place, but I had no idea except that the man I had married was changing, and I didn't know what to do.

But I tried, desperately to get a grip. The Indian nanny invited me to a Diwali ceremony on the grounds of Hughes Primary School and as I wandered about the stalls I came across a woman handing out pamphlets promoting Raja Yoga. Taking a pamphlet, I struck up a conversation with the woman, who introduced herself as Karen. It turned out that she worked at the Department of Foreign Affairs, not far from me, as I'd gone over there to work as one of the Aboriginal diplomatic trainees. The next morning, I enrolled in a Raja Yoga course at this serene (as you would hope!) meditation centre close to home, thinking this sounds as if it could help me to get more peaceful and detached from what was going on around me, especially at home.

I walked into a room bathed in a red glow. There was even a picture frame with a tiny red light in the centre. The yoga teacher talked about the spirit and the soul and how to focus the eyes during meditation. He turned the lights down and turned on soft music, pointing to the picture frame with the red light in the centre. 'Just focus your eyes on that,' he said.

So I did. And suddenly I was travelling out of my body, across this ocean of grey shimmery white light, this light at the end just pulling me across, all this love just pulling me.

From then on, every morning I wrapped six-month-old Arika in the doona I had made for her and we headed for the centre. She lay on the floor, sleeping peacefully, while I floated, calm but wrung out. When Arika was a little over a year and had finally been weaned, we started giving her chamomile tea before bedtime. One night I came home from work to find William pouring port into her bottle.

'Hey,' I barked at him, 'that's not chamomile tea!'

He shrugged. 'She goes to sleep quicker when I do this.' I grabbed her and marched off to the bedroom, yelling at him that he wasn't to put grog in her bottle!

For the first time since I met him, William was talking about the Vietnam war, probably because in the mid-1980s, 13 years after Australia's involvement in the conflict ended, everyone was finally talking about the war. There was growing public aware-ness of post-traumatic stress among Vietnam veterans, and the blockbuster movies *Platoon*, *Full Metal Jacket* and *Good Morning, Vietnam* burst onto the screen. In 1987, about two years after I caught William pouring port into the baby's bottle, the Hawke government decided the time had come for Australia to reconcile with Vietnam veterans and acknowledge they had been met with shameful indifference, even hostility, on their return from the battlefield. In October, 25,000 veterans marched in a belated Welcome Home Parade in Sydney as a large crowd cheered them on, and Prime Minister Bob Hawke announced that Long Tan Day, on 18 August, would be known as Vietnam Veterans Day.

Six years ago, a Vietnam vet called Bill Turczynski, from the southern highlands of New South Wales, recalled to a local journalist how, on the morning of 5 May 1968, the Viet Cong had struck hundreds of positions in South Vietnam; and Bill's battalion, The Royal Australian Regiment, was deployed to intercept the Viet Cong before they reached their target. Bill jumped from an army helicopter into Viet Cong territory, deep behind enemy lines.

'At that moment,' read the article in the *Southern Highland News*, 'war photographer William Errington took his photo. In the seconds it took him to click a button, he had captured the image of another fresh-faced soldier in a land far from home.'

Back in 1985, William was talking about the war, and dreaming about it.

'I feel like I'm back there all the time,' he said.

'Why don't you try writing it all down?'

But my suggestion only made things worse. Now he routinely stayed up all night, writing, a stressed and crazy look in his eyes. In the morning he showed me his work: horrible stories, the ordeal and deprivation in the jungle.

'Why don't you get some counselling,' I said. 'Why don't you come with me to the Vietnam Veterans Association?'

He refused.

Within two years of my return to work as a young mother, I found myself back at the Department of Aboriginal Affairs where Charlie Perkins was still Secretary. But again, I ran foul of Charlie's angels—his girlfriends littered the workforce—and felt the need to try something new. Karen, my meditating friend, had encouraged me to shift to foreign affairs. Who wouldn't covet a glamorous job travelling the world?

'I want to work in foreign affairs, Charlie,' I said, 'in the diplomatic service'.

Sure enough, the First Assistant Secretary at the Department set up an interview for me, and within a month my transfer came through. Meanwhile, I saw an ad in the paper for an Aboriginal woman to sit on the board of Toora, the single women's refuge; so I took up that offer, too. I was industrious. And I was now polishing off two bottles of wine a night.

In the early hours one night I awoke, startled. It was dark. My husband was groaning and sweating in his sleep.

'William, something's going wrong,' I whispered.

'You know how I told you I'd stayed faithful to my wife during the war?' Oh God, I thought. Here we go again. The new William obsessively raked over the past.

'Well that wasn't true.' He'd had an affair with an African American woman from the US army.

'I've just always loved black-skinned women.' I felt my stomach drop.

William began using cocaine. He would go to the Press Club and come home drunk, bringing some female journos with him.

'They can sleep in the spare room,' he'd say.

'William—what's this about?' He'd shrug.

For all my efforts to carve out a life different from my mother's, I was enduring the same trauma she experienced with my father when his war-time memories surfaced. Desperate for answers, I consulted a medium.

'Is my life changing?' I asked her.

She nodded. 'Something dramatic is going to happen.'

And so it did the evening I came home from work to find Arika lying in front of the open fire, William spread-eagled on the couch, snoring, an empty wine bottle on the floor. *That's it*, I thought. I bought myself a car, aptly, a Fiat Bambino, and took Arika with me everywhere. The following week, without informing William, I checked us into Beryl's, a women and children's refuge; I talked to the counsellors about psychological abuse, but made it clear I wasn't blaming William, I simply wanted to understand him.

A week later we moved into an apartment. I told William our whereabouts and said he could visit his daughter whenever he liked.

'Look, I understand you just need some space,' he said.

In the months that followed he pleaded with me to come back.

***

At the Toora refuge, where I eventually became a staff member, two addiction experts gave a talk to the women about the 12-step detox program. Listening to the experts speak, I felt a stab of recognition. Shortly afterwards one of the addiction counsellors at the refuge approached me.

'You know you're an alcoholic, don't you?'

'Is that what's wrong with me?'

But of course, I knew the answer. With a newfound clarity, I enrolled in the 12-step program and asked William to attend a meeting with me. Afterwards, he drove me to his place. We sat for a while in the car.

'Why don't you come back?' he said. 'I know you can do this, you can deal with all your problems.' As if he had no problems of his own. A door slammed shut in my mind.

'It's not going to happen, William.'

And then, tragically, William and I spiralled into bitterness, sorrow, vengeance and anger. He was terrified I'd take Arika from him, just as his first wife had deprived him of their children. Even though I insisted I would never do that, he lawyered up at the prospect, hyper-vigilant and distrustful. A custody dispute. Interim orders. At one point, William convinced my mother to sign an affidavit alleging I was a neglectful mother.

He accused me of being a drunk, citing my enrolment in the 12-step program as proof. Mad with stress, I consumed a packet of Panadol. More accusations. In photographs, I looked drawn, skinny, ghost-like. After a gruelling legal battle, we managed to set aside our rancour to nurture our daughter. We settled for joint custody; she would continue her schooling at Red Hill in Canberra.

'But when Arika starts bleeding she'll come and live with me,' I told William, 'because that's cultural'. That's when she has to start learning women's business.

Separation inevitably forces people to grapple with a new identity, but in my case personal crisis collided with political catharsis. On October 26, 1985, when the Hawke Government returned to the Anangu traditional owners the title deeds to Uluru-Kata Tjuta National Park—and the people immediately leased the land back to the Commonwealth for 99 years—I was one of the hundreds of Aboriginal people who descended on Mutitjulu to witness the hand-over ceremony. I set up camp on the red earth across the road from the mighty rock and watched as triumphant Elder, Nipper Winnmarti, brandished the deeds while his grandson, Vincent Nipper, held aloft by Reggie Uluru, punched the air with his tiny fist. The cameras snapped, an iconic image was born. We sang and danced well into the night.

The year before the 1988 Bicentennial, as the Australian government braced itself for a year of Aboriginal protest marking the 200-year anniversary of white invasion, the Tasmanian Aboriginal Centre and its Aboriginal leader, lawyer Michael Mansell, was putting together a delegation of Indigenous people from each state to travel to Libya and secure funding and support for the struggle for Aboriginal sovereignty from Colonel Gaddafi. The poet, author and activist Kevin Gilbert, was to be in the delegation, but pulled out, worried that his past imprisonment for murder[3] would

---

3   Aged 23, he killed his wife while drunk and was sentenced to life imprisonment, serving 14 years in New South Wales' jails, including in the infamous Grafton prison for 'intractables'.

focus government and media attention, and overshadow the purpose of the visit.

So, Kevin, who lived in Canberra and stage-managed all the Aboriginal rallies and protests at the tent embassy at Parliament House, asked me if I would take his place on the delegation. There was logic to his invitation: alongside Kevin, I was heavily involved in the protest movement, a regular at African National Congress and Pan African Conference solidarity demonstrations at the South African embassy, a fixture at political rallies and human rights activism, driving round in the Fiat Bambino, Aboriginal flag and banners thrusting through the sunroof.

Armed with spray cans of red, black and yellow paint—the colours of the Aboriginal flag—me and my small gang of accomplices regularly defaced the icons of colonialism around the nation's capital, like the statues of British sovereigns and soldiers around Parliament House. One night we even went down to the British High Commission on Commonwealth Avenue and sprayed the front wall with 'Colonialists Go Home'.

As you might imagine, I accepted Kevin's offer and set off to get a passport urgently. I discussed my plans for Libya with William and he discussed it with some of his journo mates. Bill Pinwill said, 'That's a good thing for her to do'. Obviously, all William's journo mates were salivating over the 'exclusive' they knew would be theirs on my return. The story was hot, after all; Hawke and Clyde Holding, the Minister for Aboriginal Affairs who had propositioned me at the Old Parliament House within minutes of introducing himself, attacked Mansell as a traitor for encouraging an Aboriginal link with Australia's enemy.

But a few weeks before we were due to leave I came down with a very bad bug and couldn't go. In retrospect I'm pretty damn grateful I was saved by the flu. Not just for the obvious reason that I would have helped legitimise a brutal dictator, but also because this spared me from a fortnight of having to fend off Michael Mansell's relentless advances—which he was renowned for.

The delegation's return was a media sensation, not least because at the airport on their return home, they presented their Aboriginal passports, issued by the 'Aboriginal Provisional Government' and newly endorsed by the Libyan regime. Officials refused them entry. The delegates were detained until they produced their Australian passports. In 1988 I, too, applied to the APG for an Aboriginal passport; it's still lying in a box in my fancy timber filing cabinet.

At this time, too, among Aboriginal women, the talk was about decolonisation and self-determination, as it was for radical white women. At the Toora refuge, the 'lesbian revolutionaries', as these white women liked to call themselves, were fervent about social justice, Indigenous rights—and their right to transform the world through obsessively re-educating their heterosexual staff who they insisted were actually closet lesbians. The lesbian staff thought of themselves as morally superior and more spiritually enlightened than all the other feminists in town because Toora had a rule that you had to be 12 months' clean and sober to work there. They held to this delusion even though all the lesbian staff were sleeping with each other, and the workplace was remarkably incestuous and dysfunctional.

A number of these women at the refuge used spiritual names from what were seen as exotic cultures—Indian, Celtic, Native American, ancient Greek—alongside their Anglo legal name, which I thought was pretty cool. I'll change my name, too, I decided; it seemed a fitting way to mark the Bicentennial celebrations of white invasion, and considerably easier than going to Libya. Enough with being an assimilated black person, enough with white-fella conditioning, with Catholicism, with trying to make myself palatable for the *migloos*.

I asked some Aboriginal women in the desert to suggest a spiritually-fitting name for me. They gave me, 'Tjanara'. So I started calling myself Tjanara Williams. A short time later I went further still, rejecting my English surname, my father's name, for Goreng Goreng, one of our clan names through intermarriage.

'Tjanara', by the way, means 'to be willing'.

10

UNIVERSITY CHALLENGE

After the divorce I found myself living in a small cottage in Lyneham, in north Canberra, with the possessions I took from the divorce: a washing machine, stereo and the piano. Arika shifted back and forth between William and me. I had stopped working, partly because the emotional stress wreaked havoc on my concentration, partly because my time in DFAT had provoked a crisis of conscience about deserting the blackfellas whose need for my expertise dwarfed that of Australia's diplomatic corps. Still, I was dragging my feet on pursuing new opportunities in Aboriginal policy, scraping by on the sole parent benefit that covered little more than rent. I turned to the Salvos for extra help as my malaise deepened.

***

But my malaise was at least a sober one. Sobriety brings painful clarity as the mind awakens and pokes around in dusty corners. Which is as close to an explanation as I can muster for what the snap decision I took during a trip to Queensland. I visited my parents in Rocky with Arika, who was four. Mum casually mentioned that Patrick, the priest I had a crush on as a teenager, was getting married.

'Yeah, well he would get married,' I said. 'That's what he always wanted, to leave the church and get married.'

'He married a nun.'

'Yeah, that's Patrick for you.' I chuckled.

'I never trusted him,' mum said. 'I was always worried when he came around here to see you.'

Something inside me shuffled.

On my way home from Rocky, I made an unscheduled stop in Brisbane and rang the Redcliffe Parish Church. I asked to speak with Father Leo Wright.

'I'm coming to visit,' I told him when he got on the line.

My friend, Colleen, was a volunteer at the church so when I arrived, we chatted over a cup of tea. Afterwards, she took Arika to play in another room while I approached Wright in the presbytery. I can't fill in many details from this day. I can't remember who told me Wright was posted here. I recall that he did not bother closing his door, and greeted me like an old friend. And just as an old friend can sense what you're about to say, Wright understood the purpose of my visit and pre-empted me.

'I remember what happened between us when you were a teenager.' He paused. 'Well, I'm sorry for that.'

I did not say much, if anything, in response. All of a sudden, my mind seized on Arika, playing nearby. *Quick*. Get out of here.

I was in this depressed state in late 1988 when my cousin, Laurel Mason, visited me from Sydney. She talked about her new job working for Linda Burney, then president of the New South Wales Aboriginal Education Consultative Group, the peak body for Aboriginal education groups around the state. Linda—who became the first Aboriginal woman to be elected to the New South Wales Parliament and more recently, the Federal House of Representatives—had secured funding to study the impact of grog, drugs and sexual abuse on the education of young girls. They were also working on an Aboriginal languages' program.

'We're looking for a qualified Aboriginal person to help us.' Laurel said, meaningfully.

I needed little convincing. A break from Canberra—perfect.

Some things are meant to be: I lodged a formal job application, flew to Sydney for the interview and was appointed 'consultant coordinator of projects' at the Aboriginal education group, with responsibility for the design, research and implementation of both programs. I had barely an inkling that I was embarking on the uneven and arduous road to self-knowledge and healing.

At first, I moved in with Laurel, who lived above a shop in Newtown. The job was based in Redfern where I set up my office and hired staff, this being a position with a lot of autonomy. The program operated in six sites around the state; for two days, Aboriginal community people from the local AECG group from the surrounding areas would gather to discuss addiction, abuse and violence. My job was to organise these meetings, facilitate the conversations and document the results. I travelled a lot, especially for the languages' program, setting up databases of Aboriginal languages so we could get funding to revive and preserve them.

So my milieu shifted dramatically from the Aboriginal political scene in Canberra, with all its ambition and in-fighting, to this tight-knit Aboriginal community in Redfern that was all family. I found myself in the orbit of Elder women: generous, wise and spirited. And just as I had leaned on such women when I travelled in the Cape during my university years, I leaned on them now. In the aftermath of a traumatic divorce, I was lost and aching, flying to Canberra fortnightly to visit Arika and hanging out for the school holidays when she'd visit me. The Elders gave me some welcome mothering—which, for many reasons, my own mother had been unable to provide for so much of my life.

Once I landed on my feet, I moved to a house in Abercrombie Street, Darlington, down the road from Redfern. As the cradle of the black power movement in the 1970s—when Aboriginal squatters and their white sympathisers squatted in the run-down terraces until the Whitlam Government intervened with a community grant to purchase real estate for Indigenous housing—Redfern, the settlement, the community hall, was a magnet for firebrands and activists. Graham Mooney managed the local community group, Aunty Maureen Watson came down from Queensland to set up the black theatre, Mick Mundine was chief of the Aboriginal Housing Company.

In the 1970s, Mundine was a foreman, directing all the building work on the Block, Redfern's restive heart. But almost 15 years later, the idealistic vision for Aboriginal empowerment was disintegrating. The Block resembled a war zone, bombed out with drug addicts and crime. As someone parachuted in to study the impact of drug and alcohol abuse on Aboriginal schooling, I did not have to venture far for case studies.

One day I was summoned to the Block, to Eveleigh Street, along with a co-worker from the program. Some of the local women came out from the terraces. The ambulance and police wanted to ask us some questions. Overnight, a five-year-old girl was raped by druggies. She was in hospital, the police explained. The women asked questions, voices rising in anger. Across the road stood two men, both of them known drug dealers. They were watching us. Some other men milled around too, shoulders slouched and eyes darting around, anxious.

'Happens all the time,' an Elder woman told me later that day. She said that trying to protect children from predators was a constant struggle.

It was the first of many shocking revelations I heard that year. At Dareton, in far west New South Wales, where we held a two-day pilot for one of our projects, women hailing from Brewarrina and Wilcannia told how every female in those towns, from little girls to adults, had been sexually abused by men of whatever skin colour; *all the women*. The welfare workers confessed privately that Wilcannia was too much hard work; the kids refused to attend school. Now I understood why this was the case, and with that knowledge came the feeling of being overwhelmed by the scale of the problem.

We had another community meeting at a park resort on the central New South Wales coast—the resort was on sacred land; you could feel the spirits there. One man, I think he was the head of some communal organisation, was a striking presence; a father in his late thirties, well-built, handsome smile, and most unusually for an Aboriginal, blonde and blue-eyed. He told the group he was stolen as a child, wrenched from his traditions, forced into 'this horrible Western culture'.

'When I get my traditional culture back, I'll get better,' he told me. 'I'll stop smoking and drinking. Stop beating my wife.'

What rubbish, I thought. Unless you get clean and sober how's your traditional culture going to help you? Unless you give up the grog, how are you going to absorb the cultural lessons about respect? There were men I knew who danced and performed ceremony in the desert and beat their wives all the same.

In the years that followed, I thought about that handsome blonde quite often. And though I never softened my views on the need for personal responsibility, I eventually came to the belief that his despair and despondency were genuine. But while some Aboriginals were beginning this painful conversation about the ubiquity of child sexual abuse in our past and present, others would have none of it. At the first New South Wales Aboriginal

Women's Conference, which I helped organise in Dubbo, Linda Burney gave a talk about the work our education group had done on addiction and abuse. There was an angry murmur in the audience. One well-known activist rose to her feet.

'This doesn't happen here!' She yelled at Linda.

The poet and activist, Joy Williams—stolen as a seven-year-old, immersed in the seedy subculture of Kings Cross in the 1960s, her name linked to petty crime and the occult—also insisted, 'No!' Williams, who had been abused her whole life and alleged a whole lot more, too, *she* said no, we have no problem with child sex abuse here.

After the conference, a group of female Elders approached me. One of them grabbed my arm. 'Thank you very much for doing this,' she said. 'It happened to us when we were younger—and we've never talked about it.'

In this period of my life one project led seamlessly to another, like question and answer. The education group's report about the impact of alcohol and domestic violence on Aboriginal girls' learning went to the minister. After a year's work with the education group, a friend secured me a job at the New South Wales Ministry of Youth Affairs where marshalling the knowledge and expertise I had gained working for Linda, I designed the Koori Youth Program to boost Aboriginal literacy, numeracy and school retention rates. The Youth Affairs Minister poured $600,000 into the project.

By now I understood that I'd never keep more kids at school if I failed to confront the deep-seated apathy, even antipathy, towards education in the Aboriginal community. Mind you, it took me a while to uncover, let alone understand, this almost nihilistic attitude. Notwithstanding my rebelliousness as a teenager, my mother managed to instill in me a love of education and the belief it could transform lives. But in 1990, I encountered the view that education was a tool to force Aboriginals to assimilate into white culture. I battled to convince people that the reverse is true, that education is a means of resisting the pull of white culture.

It was getting easier, however, to convince bureaucrats that to lift school retention rates, children needed access to Aboriginal counsellors and support staff at schools. Young kids were being physically abused at home and had no one outside the family they could safely confide in. We instituted three pilots for the Koori Youth Program; one in the mid-northern coastal town of Taree proved very successful and was written up in *The Bulletin* magazine. I wanted to spend more time in the country, with communities on the margins, so applied for a job in the Aboriginal Unit at Charles Sturt University's Bathurst campus, but didn't get it. Then the university called me back, saying I should apply for the position of overseeing the three managers of the Aboriginal Centres at all three campuses.

'We think you're more qualified for that,' they said.

So I applied, got the job and moved to Wagga Wagga, the city smack between Sydney and Melbourne, straddling the Murrumbidgee River. It was familiar territory—I'd passed through there many times in my trucking days.

The Aboriginal units at universities, including Charles Sturt, were a fairly recent innovation. The Commonwealth funded them directly, with strings attached such as employment quotas for Aborigines within the institutions. The first thing I tackled was the university's casualised Aboriginal workforce. As a committed unionist, I was appalled to learn that one of the employees, 22 years at the university and 'acting manager' Jenny Croker of the Wagga Wagga Aboriginal Centre, Ngunnagunawali, was still employed on a casual basis. In fact, all the staff were casuals, even the academics who lectured and tutored the students were employed on short-term contracts. And this was despite the university having ample capacity to provide employee security through recurrent funding via the Federal Government's three-to-five-year Aboriginal Education Strategy.

Basically, the university's employment practices were racist—at that time, staff in other departments were often employed on a permanent basis if they had been working at the university as casuals for more than two years. I knew it was essential that our staff be productive and devote their hearts and minds to the important work that lay ahead. The university had to make a commitment so that our employees would make a reciprocal commitment.

I set about identifying every non-academic position in the units, converting them all to permanent. I also found that a lot of money intended for the Aboriginal program was being siphoned off to various departments. So, I clawed the funds back. Then, I found some $60,000 lying in the coffers of student services, and lobbied the powers-that-be for what was rightfully ours.

'I'll get all the money into the Aboriginal budget and you just spend it as you should,' the Pro Vice-Chancellor told me, after my protracted campaign for greater transparency.

My duties entailed writing a three-year strategic plan.

'How do you write a strategic plan?' I asked a friend who worked as a leadership consultant.

And amid the bureaucratic wrangling, the teething problems, the inevitable in-fighting and workplace politics, loomed our biggest challenge: only about 1 per cent of the Aboriginal students who got into uni ended up finishing their course. How was I going to turn this bleak statistic around?

***

My great-grandfather, Alick Little, with his wife Frances and his family.
My grandmother, Beatrice, is top left behind Alick, circa 1925.

My parents, George and Maureen, 1950.

L to R: Peter, mum, Patricia, Kevin. In front: James and me, 1964.

L to R: Me in my Grade 3 unifrom with my sister, Patsy who was in Year 9, 1965.

Me as a bridesmaid at my sister's wedding, 1971.

After leaving teachers' college—first job, first dress, Brisbane, 1977.

My wedding, 1981.

Entering Parliament House, Canberra, after parking my Land Rover,
complete with Aboriginal flag, in the space for ministers' parking, 1981.

In Rockhampton, 6 months pregnant, 1983.

With Arika at a land rights protest, Canberra, 1987.

In front of a mural, Redfern, 1994.

With Dr Braveheart, Sioux medicine man, Minnesota, 1998.

L to R: Me, Su Anne, Kevin, Traci, Peter. Su Anne's wedding, 2001.

Su Anne at her wedding with my mum, 2001.

Me with my daughter, Arika, and my first grandchild, Willa, Canberra, 2018.

As my professional expertise developed, as a new generation of Aboriginal activists and feminists tentatively lifted the lid on the scale of violence and dysfunction in their communities, as my daughter's absence was a constant, sad presence in my life, as something I could not yet identify stirred in my consciousness, I kept looking for peace through meditation. During my time in Sydney, before the shift to Charles Sturt at Wagga Wagga, I'd set my alarm at 4 a.m. so I could make it to Raja Yoga class.

Some of the people in my class visited the Raja Yoga headquarters in Rajasthan state in northwestern India, run by three Elder women who helped the Founder establish the Brahma Kumaris University in the late 1930s. These classmates would leave as regular, harried Sydneysiders and on their return seemed transformed, glowing, as the cliché would have it. One of them told me, 'Trust us, God is coming, she's the medium for Shiva and Brahma Baba'; I thought: well this, I have to see.

The first step was paying a visit to Dr Nirmala Karjaria, a medical doctor who was also the chief administrator of the Brahma Kumaris, World Spiritual University in Australia and the Asia Pacific region. The UN-affiliated Brahma Kumaris is a religious movement originating in Hyderabad, now in Pakistan, in the 1930s, with a distinctly feminist philosophy that gives women a prominent role in the movement. As the term 'university' implies, despite their Hindu roots, the Kumaris see themselves as engaging in education rather than worship. I paid a visit to Dr Karjaria at the Raja Yoga meditation centre in Bondi which is run by two lovely 'sisters' who, some time ago, answered the call to spiritual service. One of them, Pam, said to me: 'C'mon, we'll dress you in a white sari for the meeting'.

'A white sari? You've got to be kidding!' I squeaked.

I changed into the white sari, anyway, and let them plait my hair.

'You look like an Indian princess,' Dr. Nirmala said.

Oh Lord, I thought, this is some weird cult.

In the meeting Dr Karjaria asked if I was vegetarian. I told her that I was—I'd given up eating meat since I was 21 years old, some nine years before. She said that in that case, there was one more religious requirement I had to fulfil before I could go to India: celibacy. I had already given up meat, now I just had to give up men. Which, as it turned out, wasn't really that hard.

With the proceeds of my divorce settlement, I splurged on a ticket to the subcontinent, leaving in March 1991. I went with a Melbourne friend, an actress who was a veteran visitor to the academy. Though I was 32, I felt like a complete innocent. While the trip only lasted two and a half weeks, it felt like an odyssey.

The Kumaris' world headquarters, called 'Madhuban' (meaning 'forest of honey') is located at Mount Abu, which the website accurately describes as a 'picturesque hill station'. Over the previous 15 years some foreign visitors had trickled through. My first impression was of an oriental mansion, a charming collision of serenity and kitsch. Everyone, including the mainly western international guests, wore white saris and slept in dorms. There were a lot of artists and actors. Everyone was freed from the mundane demands of their lives back home; no cooking, no cleaning, no commitments. People from the various states in India took turns each year to serve everyone in the dining halls, and the University employed local tribal women and men to do the cleaning and general maintenance, alongside the Indian men and women who worked in the University.

I befriended Alex and Anthony, both Londoners. One played the Irish drums, the other the fiddle; we jammed together, attended classes, meditated, ambled about the village, and visited a tailor for customised, and gorgeous, Indian outfits.

And then I met God.

But let me backtrack a little.

The founder of the Kumaris, Dada Lekhraj Khubchand Kripilani—the man known to us as 'Brahma Baba'—was a wealthy jeweller who, in the mid-1930s, started to have visions and transcendental experiences, believing a 'greater power' was working through him and his disciples. Those disciples came mostly from a wealthy mercantile caste; many were women and children, whose husbands and fathers travelled overseas on business. Brahma Baba not only elevated women to leadership positions in the movement, he also pushed what at the time were considered radical feminist philosophies, advocating for the right of young women not to marry, and for married women to choose celibacy. This may sound vaguely cultish, but Brahma Baba was not interested in attaching himself to women so much as in liberating them through spiritual growth.

He collected all his money and placed it in a trust to establish a university.

Unsurprisingly a committee of local men began pushing back. They picketed the movement's premises and tried to burn it down, harassing and even assaulting the women attending meetings. In 1938, Brahma Baba left the increasingly tinderbox atmosphere of Hyderabad, relocating his operations to an ashram in Karachi. The following year the government outlawed the movement, reinstating an earlier edict from a lower court, but did not enforce the ban. Brahma Baba survived an assassination attempt. In 1950, the movement shifted its headquarters again, this time to Mount Abu. When Brahma Baba died in 1969, Gulzar Dadi, one of the senior women who had been with him since she was eight, became the new medium. When she talks, the disciples believe she's channelling Shiva—'the Supreme Soul'.

Back when I visited the university, roughly every fortnight people gathered in this hall that sat five thousand, and we got to meet the medium, or, more accurately, Brahma Baba and Shiva, the two supreme souls who came together in her. And that's how I came to be confronted with the sight of Gulzar Dadi perched on a stool, while Dr. Karjaria—the doctor from Bondi—translated for her. And I was sitting there getting *drishti*, a sensation of intense concentration that lets you see into another's soul.

When the medium put out her hand to me, I could feel her touch radiating energy.

'You're an empress, are you not?' she said.

I chuckled. First an Indian princess, now an empress.

'No!'

In our classes back in Bondi, the teachers had described empresses as people of the highest principles, people serving the world. The medium kept her gaze on me.

'So, you're an empress?' she repeated.

This time I nodded, transfixed, the energy at fever pitch. I couldn't speak. For the rest of the day I did not utter a word. I felt like my soul had been extracted, processed and put back inside me. I felt encased in a bubble of golden light. But some years later, Alex told me he felt very sorry for me wondering around in a daze. He thought I looked like someone who badly needed a friend.

***

Over the years I've married the Aboriginal and Kumaris' spiritual heritage in my mind, finding synergies between the two. The Kumaris say 'don't act out of ego, lust, anger, greed'; Aboriginal culture teaches the same. Be humble, practise detachment from material possessions, from relationships; the same again. The Kumaris acknowledge and affirm other religions; they envisage a tree, with religions being its branches, each faith coming into the world at a particular time; with an iron, silver and copper age, but each seeking gold. And the higher being, or whatever you want to call him, is the seed for the tree.

The Kumaris believe the universe follows an eternal 5000-year life cycle, and at first I wondered how that tallies with the Aboriginal view that the world is 45,000 years old. But when I asked one of my Elders she said, 'Interesting you should say this, because our clan has a sacred songline, *Tjukurpa*, that's 5,000 years old.' That songline is part of the rain song that was given to me. Aboriginal cultural philosophy also talks about a cycle in the world, and about beings of golden light who spread this energy, put the law in the land, opened the songlines for us and created the sacred sites.

And both Aboriginals and the Kumaris believe that the higher being is grounded in our physical bodies; when we die, the spirit dies with us. When the nuns at school intoned that 'God is everywhere, your soul is everywhere,' I could never quite swallow the idea. For me, God—*Biaime*—is always rooted in a particular place, the place from which our ancestors were sent and the place to which they returned. And that's why you can sit in the bush and commune with your ancestors.

In the decades following that trip to India, I gave workshops showing how the two cultures are connected. I guess you could say I've become an expert at merging disparate cultures and schools of thought—after a while you get practised at all kinds of reconciliation.

I have Raja Yoga to thank for many adventures: travel, study, meeting amazing people, engaging in fascinating conversations, contributing to peacekeeping efforts around the world. I ran programs and workshops on art, addiction, spirituality and consciousness-raising. Even if I suspend some beliefs in aspects of the Kumaris' faith, the creed has broadened my perspective on the world, taken me beyond my small Aboriginal milieu, and tapped into a more universal experience. And during the difficult years that followed my return from India, Raja Yoga proved a constant source of comfort.

One year I took one of my Elders who had taught me women's business, to the first World International Women's conference at Mount Abu. She loved it.

'Let's make Aboriginal saris,' she said.

Before we left for India we had bought six yards of fabric, decorated with Aboriginal motifs from a shop in Parramatta and packed it in the suitcase. Now I wrapped the cloth around her, sari style.

11

TOUCHING SHAME

'When you touch shame it's very hard to face.'

And here I was, in the autumn of 1993, two years after my first spiritual encounter in India, with the guru-like philosopher, counsellor and theologian, John Bradshaw, at his eponymous clinic at Rosemead Hospital in Los Angeles, where he diagnosed my people's suffering and my own, even if I was yet to fully confront the latter.

Bradshaw had thoroughly interrogated his childhood trauma and come up with answers that made it onto the bestseller lists. He grew up fatherless in Houston, Texas: abandoned by his alcoholic father, who was in turn abandoned by *his* alcoholic father. As a young adult, he joined the seminary and began studying for the priesthood, gaining bachelor's and master's degrees in psychology, philosophy, and theology from St Michael's College at the University of Toronto. But his genes caught up with him, as he, too, developed a drinking problem. He left the seminary a few days before being ordained.

A few weeks before Christmas 1965, he admitted himself into Austin State Hospital for alcohol treatment. Within years of his release, he was a talk-show regular, prolific writer and a pioneer of the self-help movement. When he died in 2016, an obituary in the *Houston Chronicle* said he'd been more than 50 years sober, abstaining from drink one day at a time. His books, such as *Healing the Shame that Binds You*, about alcoholics and their children, and intergenerational shame and dysfunction, really spoke to me because they were highly relevant to my work with Aboriginal communities.

I came to be at his workshops via a friend from the 12-step program in Brisbane, who had asked me and some therapists if we wanted to attend Bradshaw's training in Non-Shaming Therapy in LA. Bradshaw was also doing workshops across California, helping people with a history of addiction and violence in their family of origin to defeat their own addictions. We were taught how to use narrative therapy, psychodrama, role playing—the therapeutic techniques then in vogue. In the process of doing all of that, you write stories about your own life. To be a therapist, the thinking goes, you have to deal with your own issues first so that you don't get them tangled with your client's.

So at this workshop I was forced to sit down and write about my own issues. My own shame.

On the surface, my life at the time was not dysfunctional. I was nearly six years sober, and after nearly three years in the job at Charles Sturt, we had overwhelmingly met the challenge to ensure that more than a miserable 1 per cent of Aboriginal students completed their university degrees. By the end of 1993, retention rates soared to 93 percent. All we did was create a pathway from high school to university, and establish a network of family support, bringing in people who could be aunties and uncles to the university students. We invited Aboriginal students who were collecting the ABSTUDY benefit to meet with us at the faculty, sit tests and go before an interview panel. We saw that improving outcomes was a collaborative exercise. My interest in high-level education policy grew; I was a national rep on the National Aboriginal and Torres Strait Islander Educational Policy Committee.

The same year, a body called the National Aboriginal Higher Education Network hosted their annual conference at Hervey Bay on the Queensland coast. We were mainly people in universities—Aboriginal academics embarking on postgraduate degrees, rather than bureaucrats or policy workers. Some of the women talked about Aboriginal kids at school, in particular, the poor retention rates, and the fact that children weren't learning. The answers were obvious to me, given everything I had encountered and read. 'Well,' I thought to myself, 'the kids aren't getting fed. They go home every day to find their parents fighting each other, he's getting drunk, beating the shit out of her...'

My colleagues were asking: 'Why can't the parents get involved with the school?' I knew why: they were too caught up with what was going on at home, with survival—the lack of money—why would they turn up at a white school to see what's happening? Such a ridiculous expectation from white schoolteachers—that Aboriginal parents come and talk to them when they're not even talking to each other; when she's got a black eye, when she's not going out in public. But none of my colleagues wanted to talk about this. No, they wanted to theorise about education, pedagogy and curriculum.

I also wanted to talk about the intergenerational legacy of addiction, about alcohol abuse—how the behaviour of adults impacts on children. Strange as it may sound, few people were exploring such themes from an Aboriginal perspective. Through my involvement in the 12-Step program I was seeing how alcoholism affected white people; so many alcoholics were the children of alcoholics, witnesses to domestic violence, survivors of abuse.

I figured, the same thing is happening with us, it cannot be any different. Same chemicals, same behaviour. Well, not exactly the same thing; in the case of Aboriginal dysfunction you had to factor in the trauma from colonisation. Decades later these realisations led me to conclude that curing the distress of Indigenous communities required both Western psychotherapy and the spiritual prescriptions in traditional culture. I was reading voraciously. Reading and writing about addiction, families, racism, dependency and loss. I was particularly inspired by the work of family therapist Jane Middelton-Moz on Canadian Indian reservations; she was writing about precisely the same things that were exercising my mind. She observed how children of acculturation, the Indigenous children forced to assimilate to the dominant culture of the coloniser, have similar behavioural traits as children of alcoholics.

Again, a light went off in my head: 'It's the same here!' So I started referencing Middelton-Moz in my own work, which didn't please everyone in Aboriginal academia—a fact I found revealing. When, at the Healing Our Spirit Worldwide Conference in Sydney in the early 1990s, I delivered a paper that asserted the intergenerational legacy of alcoholism was part of our story, the Aboriginal activist, Michael Anderson, objected from the audience.

I revisited my theories about the Aboriginal men I had encountered years before, such as that blonde-haired, blue-eyed man from the meeting on the New South Wales central coast, who affirmed traditional law but still bashed their women. These men, I concluded, were traumatised, denying their behaviour, partly as a defence mechanism to ward off their own memories of trauma, childhood abuse and racism. I read more and more about the violence of colonisation, its impact on people's experience and behaviour; of how the victims of violence became perpetrators of violence, and how a vicious cycle of violence and dysfunction became ingrained in Indigenous communities.

The violence even seeped into the realm of traditional culture, with men bending the law to accommodate and justify their behaviour. Men blessed with every chance to live spiritually authentic lives were torn apart—split—by drugs, alcohol and the lingering trauma of childhood abuse. I guess it's similar to the way paedophile priests appear devout in public, but in private, sexually abuse children. So, I was one of a growing number of Indigenous academics researching these themes of colonisation and dysfunction, asking: 'How did our culture go from *that* to *this?*' And now, at John Bradshaw's LA clinic, pen in my hand, I was asking myself one or two painful questions about memory and shame.

I wrote. For the first time, I documented the crimes inflicted on me during childhood. How my father slapped me when I was singing and moaning in my sleep. How I was forced to sleep in the laundry on the camp bed with the dogs, engulfed by the darkness, the door to the house locked. How I whimpered, like a dog, at the front door to no avail. And then, Father Leo Wright...

The words poured out of me, overwhelmed me. I wrote for four weeks, even after returning home to Wagga Wagga from the States. I took more leave from Charles Sturt. Bradshaw was right; shame is very hard to face. But it's much easier to face in a safe environment on the other side of the world where no one was around to deny your ordeal.

I did artwork. I meditated. I took long walks by the Murrumbidgee River. Memories surfaced. Childhood. Divorce. Arika. God, how I missed her. Missed seeing her grow day by day.

Sadness washed over me.

***

Despite my achievements at Charles Sturt, the job wore me down. I was constantly fighting with them over the budget, the strategic plan and every other thing, which left me feeling they did not value or understand our unit's work. In truth, I was over being a university administrator, it became a constant grind and I was becoming emotionally incapable of working such long hours; I needed a break.

A friend at Sydney University, who was director of the Aboriginal unit, an academic research and teaching unit, asked if I wanted a job there. 'Yes,' I said.

So, I moved back to western Sydney, taking up residence in a small terrace in Nelson Street, Annandale. I acquired a cat. Arika visited every fortnight.

I thought afresh about my future—and past. In my early adulthood, drinking and drug-taking hampered my efforts to obtain a degree, though in the intervening years I'd still managed to carve out a field of research, from outside academia. The Sydney Uni gig got me focused on academia again. I figured I'd finally complete that last year of my undergraduate Arts degree by tackling one subject at a time; so I enrolled at Charles Sturt through distance education. At Sydney Uni, meanwhile, I taught Aboriginal studies to undergraduates in the medical and educational faculties; we also offered a teaching diploma for Aboriginal students. Students came from around the country. A tide of hope was sweeping through Aboriginal Australia: the previous year, in response to the High Court's momentous Mabo decision, the Keating government enshrined Indigenous land and property rights in the Native Title Act—then law student, Noel Pearson, one of Sydney Uni's own, had been part of the core negotiating team with the prime minister.

That's not to say the Aboriginal unit at Sydney Uni was entirely functional and harmonious. I would stay there for one productive year, only slightly marred by internal politics and animosity between colleagues.

As that year drew to an end, my mental health frayed yet again. I had never been one for sleeping in total darkness; I liked looking out at the trees, their branches white under the street lamps. But now, every night I drew the curtains in the terrace house, holding myself tight in the blackness. In October, flashbacks ambushed me. Leo Wright, over and over. Now, to fall asleep I needed the light on.

Driving back from Double Bay one afternoon, down Edgecliff Road, past Rushcutters Bay, I found myself gasping for air. I turned into a side street, pulled over, scrambled out of the car.

Where was I?

A tree. Yes. Something organic.

I planted myself on the nature strip, my back against the tree, heart pounding, hyperventilating, hands clasping at the grass.

'You're having a breakdown,' said my friend, at the other end of the line. A prominent addiction psychologist and fellow veteran from Bradshaw's workshop, he worked at a private drug and alcohol therapeutic clinic. He said I should admit myself to the clinic as an inpatient. I returned to work and requested four weeks off to go to the clinic.

In the clinic they practised emotional release therapy, group therapy; inviting us to regress into a scene. The catharsis got me on a high, flooded with endorphins! This feeling, of intense healing, can be addictive too. I stayed at the clinic for a month. But afterwards, I still couldn't work, routines still defeated me. I waited out the end of my contract at Sydney Uni and decided I couldn't go back to full-time work. I hid in bed with the doona over my face.

As the calendar flipped into a new year, 1995, I made another pilgrimage to India, and came back, as always, partially renewed. I moved in with a friend in Glebe while I hunted for a new apartment in Ashfield so I could live close to the Raja Yoga centre. I enrolled in a couple of subjects at Sydney Uni, still chasing, in a lacklustre way, that elusive Arts degree. Otherwise, my plans were vague. 'Well,' I thought, 'I'll get an apartment out near the main centre at Ashfield and I'll focus on my spiritual life, and then perhaps I'll get a job and let's see.'

It was in this meandering state, in February 1995, that one morning, craving light entertainment, I bought the latest edition of *Who*. Returning to my friend's place in Glebe, I sat down at a desk by the window in the spare room, flipped open the magazine and began leafing through.

12

'WE'VE GOT A BIG FILE ON HIM.'

Reeling, I absorbed the double-page spread about the former Ballarat priest, Gerald Risdale, sentenced the previous year in Melbourne's County Court to 18 years' jail for child sex offences. (His tally of convictions and jail terms has since soared after more victims came forward—Risdale will almost certainly die in prison.)

You can put them in jail!

At the bottom of the story there was a note, to the effect of 'if this happened to you, contact the Catholic victims' support group, Broken Rites'.

'This happened to me,' I told the man at the other end of the line.

'If you don't mind me asking,' he said, 'can you tell me who the priest was because we keep lists and we do investigation stuff, background stuff.'

'It's Father Leo Wright.'

'We've got a big file on him.'

As it happened, the man explained, the police were in the middle of an investigation into Leo Wright. He said there were

113

three other victims, two sisters and a boy, who all knew each other. The allegations related to Wright's time at Manly parish— way before I crossed paths with him. He said the police wanted to find someone else, another victim, who did not know the others. Would it be okay if he passed on my name, so the police could contact me?

'Yes,' I said, my mind strangely blank.

Three others. A big file.

I hung up the receiver, wiped the conversation from my mind and got on with my day.

A couple of weeks later, shortly after I moved into an apartment in Ashfield, a few doors down from the Raja Yoga centre, a Detective Walsh, from taskforce something or rather, called.

'Would you be willing to give us a statement?' he asked.

The police station at Strawberry Hills, near Redfern, was an imposing grey building with green-tinted glass. I told no one that I was making the trip. I did not think of lining anyone up to give me emotional support, I did not think at all. In a further sign of my naiveté, I assumed the process would take a few hours. It took two days.

I sat opposite a male and female detective. The man wore a shirt and tie—no suit. The policeman smiled a lot.

'Take your time,' they said, 'it's okay'. 'Do you need somebody here with you?'

'Another cup of tea?' Never before had coppers been so nice to me.

Somewhat unnerved by the rigour and specificity of the detectives' questions, I told them the whole story, from the age of 13 through to 18. The bus journey from Rockhampton to Melbourne for the 40th International Eucharistic Congress. The corroboree at Werribee. The attempted rape at my place in Hill End in Brisbane when I was 18.

Memories and feelings pierced through the frozen surface. The homesickness and isolation when I started boarding school, how much I wanted to be at the same boarding school as my sister in Brisbane, how I hated the nuns. How during that first year at boarding school, when my parents still lived at Longreach, I didn't even go home on the holidays. How I wasn't even allowed to express my feelings in letters home because the nuns made us copy what they wrote on the blackboard.

And how Leo Wright was always there: attentive when I was starving for attention, friendly when I was aching with loneliness, grooming me when I was a messed-up, hormonal teenager dreaming of romance.

The coppers said: 'Well we can't charge him with rape for the last incident because you were 18'.

I didn't entirely understand their point, but after two days of re-living nauseating memories I no longer cared what they were doing. I thanked them, departed from the police station, caught the train back to Ashfield, curled up in bed and pulled the doona over my head.

'We'll organise a flight to Queensland so you can give evidence in court,' said Detective Walsh on the phone.

Every morning I woke at 4 a.m. Meditated. Went to the 6 a.m. Raja Yoga class, and from there, still wearing my white sari, to my friend, John's house, across the road. We drank chai and talked about my life goals; he was coaching me in 'self-managing leadership'. We plotted charts of my aspirations—in the following years I managed to tick off a number of items as mission accomplished. But back then I struggled through persistent fog. I attended the odd uni lecture in first semester; by second semester the fog overwhelmed me, so I didn't enrol. Every now and then

Arika visited; every now and then I travelled to Canberra to visit her. I did not work. Long hours dissolved, with the doona pulled over my head.

Around September, Detective Walsh called again. Good news: Leo Wright was pleading guilty; I was spared from giving evidence in court. I remember thinking, 'Ah well, that's karma at work; he has to have it settled. He knows he's guilty.' Later, I heard that Wright claimed he'd pleaded guilty to save us all the 'distress' of having to give evidence.

By then, he was charged over offences against five victims, including me: a boy aged 14, and three girls, two of them younger than 12 at the time. The back story to this chapter has since become a matter of public record. One of the victims, a non-Aboriginal woman called 'Mary', was assaulted by Wright when she was 10; when her own daughter approached her 10th birthday, she was compelled to report the crime to the Brisbane archdiocesan authorities.

Three years later, in 1993, Mary found that Wright was still practising as a priest in the parish house at Tugan on the Gold Coast. So she lodged a police report. The church responded the following year by sending Wright to the St Luke Institute, a clinic for sexually abusive priests in the US. Wright's lawyers say he will-ingly became an inpatient at St Luke, having publicly confessed his problems at a meeting when St Luke's director toured Australia; they also claim he had confessed his sex crimes to a bishop in 1972, and again, to a different bishop, in 1993. On both occasions he was transferred to a new parish, no other action taken.

Mary knew none of this, and she never heard back from the police. In mid-1995, she saw Wright listed as a priest in the official Catholic directory. Incensed, she contacted police to reactivate her complaint. This time police sought out more victims.

I also learned that the prosecution had intended to subpoena two top archdiocesan clerics to be questioned in court about their prior knowledge of Wright's offences, but his guilty plea made this unnecessary. That sorry chapter, about the Church's complicity and cover-up, was told two years later, when more evidence of Wright's depravity came to light.

I resolved to fly to Brisbane, to see Wright sentenced in the dock. As I was waiting in the Qantas Club, a journalist called me. The detective had asked me earlier if I was willing to speak to the media; I suppose I must have said, yes.

'Is there anything you'd like to say?' the journalist asked.

I dithered.

As the sentencing neared, I imagined the media-packed courtroom and my nerve failed me. I felt vulnerable, frightened of exposure. I stayed away.

Wright was sentenced in December 1995 to three years. It was big news: the first Catholic priest to be jailed for child sex offences in Queensland. The media reported he was sentenced for offences committed between 1968 and 1977 against three children and an 18-year-old Aboriginal woman. Me.

After the case, Brisbane's archdiocesan chancellor, the Very Reverend Dr James Spence, said Wright remained a priest and after serving his time he would be accepted back into the ministry.

You can put them in jail.

He is in jail.

Was he really in jail? For reasons I can't fully explain, I had to be certain.

Brisbane's remand centre was adjacent to the city court house; an old building with paint peeling on the walls. Half-dazed, I drove there the day after Wright's sentencing. I rocked up to the front office and asked to see him. I last set eyes on him eight years ago at the Redcliffe presbytery, when he said, 'I'm sorry for that'. Was he more sorry now?

The copper escorted me in the lift. We approached a corridor with cells.

'He's in here.'

At first, I saw a woman in her late 40s, early 50s, blonde, tidy, typically Queensland Catholic. The pair were standing in the corridor, chatting. Behind them, an open cell; prison bars, a single bed alongside a melancholy green-grey wall. This time Wright was not wearing his regulation white shirt and black pants. His prison garb matched the walls, green-grey. Tracksuit pants—grey. My eyes lingered on the grey tracksuit pants.

He jolted at the sight of me, but when he spoke the tone was arrogant.

'Hello, Pam… This is…'—a polite gesture at the woman, 'my counsellor'.

I had expected to see him beaten, whimpering in his cell. Not this sanctimony, this 'I'm doing my sacred duty to reconcile myself with God' routine. I stood, staring at them. I felt the presence of a third person in the room—my confused and needy teenage self. At last, I spoke.

'I just came to make sure you're in jail.'

Wright flung open his arms and walked towards me. The woman smiled. My God—he was going to hug me. I stepped back. He stopped in his tracks. I turned around and left.

Though I was still shaking when I returned to the car, another feeling was overtaking me, and it closely approximated happiness.

***

I returned to Sydney, settled back into normal life and flew to a Raja Yoga conference in Sardinia in the summer. Maybe it was no coincidence that after the conference when I travelled to Milan to do some other workshops and I stayed with my friend Laura who managed the Raja Yoga Centre there, I met Enrico, the deputy mayor of Orta San Giulio, a beautiful mediaeval town northwest of the city on Lake Orta. Enrico had a shock of white hair, a sharp sense of humour and lived with his elderly mother in an old stone two-storey cottage on a hillside in town. He invited me to stay with him and, due to his rank, I had the best access of any tourist to the local sites. At the 12th-century Romanesque Benedictine monastery in the middle of the lake on Isola San Giulio, the fishing boats bobbed on the shoreline and the nuns sang Vespers ethereally. It was a magical place. I went to Orta regularly over a three-month period, staying with a friend of Laura's who owned a dress shop there. She and her little girl lived in a quaint mediaeval townhouse by the water.

On the way back from Italy, I went to Denmark where I'd been invited to hold a workshop on Aboriginal women's business with women from there, some of whom had attended the international women's conference at the Brahma Kumaris' headquarters in India. This is where I first sensed that Western women were grieving for their lost womanhood or femininity within a male-dominated world. Many of these women needed healing, not because social progress was too slow but because it was too fast. In Danish society, men had become like 'little boys', they told me. The men were increasingly staying home to look after the kids while the women were the main breadwinners. The society was undergoing a major power shift between the sexes, a welcome shift, and yet the women confessed their feelings of ambivalence.

'I feel like my husband has given up,' one of the women said. Another woman admitted a yearning for masculinity in her husband; the social revolution sat awkwardly with the nation's Viking heritage, she explained. Other women were looking for a deeper connection with the earth, with their ritual past, requesting me to do ceremonies. And so, I did.

Since then I've delivered hundreds of such workshops in Australia and overseas, tapping into women's suppressed longing for closeness with each other, for a connection with earth, for a deeper understanding of their nation's Indigenous cultures. While I was leading a workshop at the University of Western Australia later that year, a visiting professor from St Catherine's College, Minnesota, invited me to do the same at her university's annual 'soul conference'.

So in September, I flew to St Paul, Minnesota, which was still covered in snow—the professor had to lend me her winter coat and shoes. My workshop on Aboriginal spirituality, law and culture attracted 900 people, mostly environmental science types and New-Age, conflicted Catholics.

I gave a separate talk at a local Mass, the congregation gathered in a school sports' hall as a symbolic protest to the Catholic Church about homelessness, vowing not to hold Mass in their church until all the city's homeless were housed. As I spoke about the three laws of respect, I caught sight of a group of native Americans in the back row and felt a stab of sadness for them; their history was so similar to my mob's, but here was I up on a pedestal because, as an Aboriginal, I was lauded as coming from the oldest culture on earth.

After my sermon, the congregants came up for Holy Communion. One of the native American women from the Owjibwa approached me. Taking a black-and-white feather out of her hair and smiling radiantly, she handed it to me.

***

At the end of that year, just before Christmas, Arika, fresh out of primary school, came to live with me, as envisaged in my agreement with William. She had started bleeding; it was time to be with her mother.

13

'WHY WOULD A PRIEST DO THIS?'

In the three years following Leo Wright's conviction, I learnt a bitter lesson: putting him in jail was the easy part. Getting the Church to acknowledge its moral culpability in his crimes and make restitution was much harder. We survivors are still fighting that battle.

The year after Wright's sentencing, the Church's silence gnawing at me, I went to see Sydney bishop, Geoffrey Robinson, who was spearheading the Church's anti-abuse response, and was himself a victim of child sex abuse—though not by a priest—a trauma he suppressed 'up in the attic' for 50 years. Nearly 10 years earlier, Bishop Robinson attended a meeting where he heard two priests document the scale of the child sex abuse problem, a revelation that set him on a crusade for justice for victims and for radical Catholic reforms, including scrapping obligatory celibacy. (Two decades after my encounter with him during the Royal Commission into institutional responses to child sexual abuse, Bishop Robinson slammed Pope John Paul II and Pope Francis for lack of leadership in the Church's response to victims.)

'Should I get a lawyer?' I asked the bishop.

'The first thing you should do is visit the Archbishop of Brisbane,' he said.

'Wynberg' New Farm, in Brunswick Street, Brisbane, is a stately 19th-century residence and home, since 1928, to successive archbishops. I walked up a long, winding path alongside manicured lawns—did I note at the entrance the white marble fountain, the winged statue a replica of a work by Verrocchio? After I was escorted to a room and asked to wait, I found myself staring at a walking stick and umbrella leaning inside a holder. Don't ask me why, I can still summon a sharp image of that walking stick and umbrella, today.

Archbishop John Battersby was a short man with glasses and gingery hair and wore the clerical garb of black pants and white shirt. He invited me into his office which was a huge room with an imposing desk, couches and bookshelves. I swallowed. I explained I was one of Leo Wright's victims.

'Yes, I know who you are,' he said.

'Well I've come to talk to you because I haven't heard anything from any of you. None of you have asked if I'm okay, or have offered to do anything. He's been in jail for almost a year. I know I'm entitled to at least an apology.'

In the pause that followed, I heard music playing in the background.

'I like that music,' I said. We talked briefly about Celtic folk music.

'Well,' he resumed, 'we're not really required to do anything. I thought I'd listen to you because you're a victim, and it's my job to look after your pastoral care.'

'You're joking, right?'

'No. Are you a Catholic?'

'No, I'm not a Catholic.'

'We want to bring you back into the fold.'

He proceeded to lob questions at me. What did I do? Where did I grow up? Who were my parents? Did I have a Catholic upbringing?

Anger surged through me.

'I spent 12 years in a Catholic school. My mother gave her life to the Catholic Church. You have a responsibility to do something for my mother.'

He returned to the subject of Leo Wright.

'I just cannot believe it's true.'

'He's in jail. It *is* true. How can you sit there and be in denial?'

He said the Church was still thinking about its response, but that he had placed a bishop, John Gerry, in charge of these matters. I should have a conversation with Bishop Gerry; he would arrange for him to contact me. The Archbishop shook his head. I noticed, with shock, his eyes welling with tears.

'We do not understand why a priest would do this.'

***

At long last a plan formed in my mind. Arika and I would move back to Queensland. I would dedicate my energy to getting justice and compensation. I would return to university, and the Church would pay for my tuition. Arika wanted to go to boarding school, so they would pay for her tuition too.

And to be brutally frank, there was another compelling reason for the move. Throughout 1996, I had been working in Sydney's CBD for several state government departments. Each day I drove my car into the city centre and parked, deliberately, under some shady trees in the Supreme Court judges' car park. Like clockwork, each day bequeathed me a new parking ticket. Nonchalantly, I stashed them in the glovebox, an interim home before they ended up in the rubbish at home. As I saw it, the white authorities hadn't paid the rent on stolen land and I resented the judges' privilege of a free car park.

Which is precisely what I told the magistrate when, 15 months later, I was hauled before the Local Court for unpaid parking infringements amounting to … let's just say, a five-figure sum.

'When you pay the rent,' I told the courtroom, 'I'll pay the fines'.

A stunned silence. The magistrate grinned.

'Ms Goreng Goreng, I completely understand your sentiments, however you, like everyone else in Australia, live under Australian law and if you park illegally you get fined.'

He gave me 200 hours of community service. In the ensuing correspondence with the sheriff's office about the details, I requested to serve my punishment at an Aboriginal organisation, and thus I ended up at an Aboriginal welfare service in Ashfield. When I turned up for my first day, the manager told me to sign their log book 200 times on 200 different dates over the coming six months, then made me mop the kitchen floor, gave me a cuppa and sent me home for good.

It seemed a neat resolution until the sheriff's office phoned, claiming I hadn't completed my 200 hours—most likely the Aboriginal service messed up the paperwork—and followed up with a letter threatening to seize my furniture. Time to skip town, I reckoned.

At the time, Arika was doing her first year of high school at Leichhardt Secondary College in Sydney. Shortly after she had moved in with me, I thought, 'Well, I've got a kid now. I need an income so I can buy her things she needs.' In the paper, I saw a job advertisement for a co-ordinator of an Aboriginal women's employment career development strategy at the Department of Women. Three days a week—a perfect gig, rewarding and nurturing. But then I decided that even though Arika was doing okay at Leichhardt, I wanted to send her to a private school because I felt that I'd had a quality education and I wanted that for her too. I had recently done a consulting project at Kincoppal School, a Catholic school in Rose Bay, Sydney, and was impressed with their commitment to social justice and Aboriginal education. But for that, I would need even more money. So, I applied for a job at the NSW Attorney General's department as the director of the Aboriginal unit, and soon enough I was looking after their Indigenous justice and employment policies across the state, overseeing the Aboriginal Justice Advisory Committee. For almost a year the wheels turned smoothly enough—until, another breakdown of sorts.

I recall a meeting with a senior department official, perhaps 10 years my senior, a man with an arrogant manner. We were discussing programs to deliver more employment opportunities for Indigenous people within the department.

'And here we are with another Aboriginal person,' he said, almost groaning. 'What are you going to do? What difference is it going to make? I'm not going to give any affirmative action jobs to Aboriginals.' As if we were all dim-witted incompetents without degrees.

Unfortunately, he was not an isolated case; this apathy and contempt for the Aboriginal agenda permeated the department. And I simply ran out of emotional capacity to deal with these idiots.

'I don't want to work here, anymore; I don't like this place,' I told my boss soon after that meeting. 'I'm going home to Queensland. Seeya later.'

We moved to Russell Island in southeast Queensland and Arika boarded at Kincoppal School, where she could more easily travel between me and William, who had since moved to the south coast of New South Wales. A year later though, Arika was sick of being so far away from me, and I was struggling to pay the fees, so she returned to Queensland, eventually boarding at Ipswich Grammar School. I moved into Brisbane as I wanted to be closer to the Australian Catholic University where

I was enrolled in a postgraduate degree, and to the Raja Yoga Centre.

We found a small cottage in Fairfield on the river and I asked my mum to come down for a visit. George had had a stroke six years earlier, losing the use of his right side—and his memory. Sitting in our lounge room one day, I said to her: 'Leo Wright—do you remember him?'

Yes, she remembered him.

'Well, I was in that court case.'

A pause.

'Were you in love with him?'

'Mum, I was 13! For God's sake, he was grooming me.'

Did she remember the time she found Wright instructing me and my friend Margaret Smith how to use the photocopying machine at Yeppoon during one of the Aboriginal and Torres Strait Islander Catholic Council meetings; the three of us alone in a room? She pulled us out of there, trembling with anger, practically pushing me down the stairs? And she turned and hissed something at him?

'Oh yeah, I remember.' Then after a pause, mum asked: 'Did he do things later?'

'Well, yes.'

Mum turned her head away.

'Well, I've been talking to the Church about compensation. One of the things I want them to do is for you to have a meeting with the Bishop so he can apologise to you directly because of all the effort you put into my education and because the abuse interfered with it.'

'Okay.'

I have a hazy memory of my first meeting with Bishop Gerry, the cleric handling abuse cases in Queensland. He echoed the Archbishop's bafflement about Wright—'We don't understand why Leo did this, how this could happen?'—and so on. Like he was in some kind of fugue.

The year earlier, in 1996, Melbourne Archbishop George Pell had set up the Church's Melbourne Response to investigate and assess allegations of child sexual abuse and deliver compensation to victims. The Brisbane Archdiocese had no such process, and the Church leadership was scrambling for case-by-case solutions, although from time to time Bishop Gerry rang to assure me they were working on establishing their own procedures. I told him what I wanted—two years' salary, as I had to give up my job, and Arika's fees at school.

'Okay, I'll go and talk to them,' the Bishop said.

My academic fees for the Australian Catholic University in Brisbane, where I enrolled in a year-long postgraduate counselling course, were paid swiftly. Bishop Gerry said we had to negotiate about the school fees. I said: 'It's a Catholic school; all you do is write a cheque'.

Not knowing how long the process would take, I applied for ABSTUDY for Arika. The benefit covered the first few terms; and I paid the rest with my numerous credit cards.

For a subsequent meeting with Bishop Gerry I organised a mediator, a Jungian therapist who was an ex-nun married to an ex-priest. We got off to a tense start.

'You're not getting anything,' he said.

I knew I had to proceed carefully; my barristers had advised me that I couldn't sue the Catholic Church as my claim was outside the Statute of Limitations and the Church, with its myriad of legal entities, could not be legally sued. On the other hand, I had an emotive message that I insisted on sharing with every bishop I met from Sydney to Townsville, hinting I was prepared to share it with the media too: this is the UN's decade of Indigenous reconciliation, and here I am, to be reconciled with—

an Aboriginal woman who had helped put Queensland's first convicted paedophile priest behind bars (two firsts, there).

By the end of this meeting with Bishop Gerry we had agreed on a compensation package: the Church would pay for the costs of a healing ceremony; the Church agreed to publish in the *Koori Mail* an apology to me, my family and the extended community; and a separate apology would be given in person from a member of the clergy to my mother. At a later meeting, where I was represented by my barrister, we negotiated a lump sum payment: too small. Needless to say, all of the above was contingent on me signing a thick deed of release. At first the deed included a clause that, save for a doctor, therapist or priest, I was not to tell anyone about the abuse.

'I'm not signing this shit,' I said. In the end, the only thing I agreed to keep confidential was the settlement itself.

In the intervening years, the Church's legalistic approach to child sex abuse claims came under intense criticism for privileging the institution's reputation and assets above the pastoral and spiritual needs of victims. So, I no longer consider myself bound by the confidentiality provisions in my settlement. All bets are off.

Before my mum's meetings with Bishop Gerry, I urged her: 'You tell him how much this hurts you, mum. You tell him straight up.' The two conferred in private, as per the agreement. Precisely what each said to the other, I'll never know.

In September that same year, 1997, Leo Wright, while still incarcerated for his crimes against me and the others, pleaded guilty to charges of indecent assault and indecent dealing involving another Aboriginal girl, 'Sally', who he abused from 1970 to 1976, from the time she was 12 years old till she was 18. He had assaulted her at the Aboriginal community at Cherbourg near the town of Murgon where he was ministering. Sometimes he assaulted her immediately after conducting Mass. He continued a sexual relationship with her after she turned 18, but no criminal charges were laid over this conduct. For this abuse, he was sentenced to a further 8 months' jail, suspended after six months. It was during this hearing in Brisbane's District Court that the public was told that the Church first learnt of Wright's offending 25 years earlier. But clearly, they had turned a blind eye to it and had allowed him to remain in close contact with children.

Recently, another childhood friend told me Leo Wright started abusing her when she was 13. She said he was adamant that all he did was touch young people up, fondle them; that there was never any 'skin-to-skin' contact. As if desisting from skin-to-skin contact makes the fondling okay. And, anyway, since when is touching someone's vagina not 'skin-to-skin'?

Counter-intuitive as it may sound, at around this time I started going to church again—not for the religious affirmation but in search of healing and connection. I had recently reconnected with my old high school friend, Jeannie who was married, with two children around the same age as Arika. Now a level-headed adult, Jeannie suggested I attend her church, a radical, somewhat hippy, congregation in south Brisbane.

'We do things differently there,' she told me. 'I'll talk to the priest. Why don't you come and talk about what happened with Leo Wright, because everyone's talking about it, but no one really knows the truth. You could give the sermon.'

The church was indeed loosely anarchic; an 800-strong congregation, but the two priests, Father Terry and Father Peter, weren't exclusively in charge. Father Terry had fathered a child, a boy then aged 10. Father Peter was similarly out there. They practised Buddhist meditation. They used this big tree as a table, and everyone stood around in the middle and did Mass together. We sat on the floor. We sang. And different people gave sermons each week. I talked about Aboriginal law and how a lot of Indigenous people had been abused in Catholic institutions. I talked about my own trauma, feeling affirmation and acceptance in return.

At night, homeless Aboriginals wandered up from the parks at the river's edge. The church opened the gates and gave them sleeping bags, swags, blankets and pillows. The homeless slept on the church grounds, and in the car park shed out the back where church workers laid down mattresses for them.

Meanwhile, I had moved to Brisbane. Arika was still away at boarding school and was happy there. A friend from Raja Yoga, Ray, lived near the uni, so I would stay with him overnight, attend classes the next day and catch the ferry home. I resumed drawing and writing, walked the dog, swam in the ocean, watched the boats go by.

And yet I still wasn't well.

My wardrobe heaved with so many dresses and outfits. Every other day I changed my appearance to match my increasingly erratic personality: an innocent angel in white lace and floral patterns; a lesbian with short hair and overalls. This wasn't exactly new; there were other times in my life when I engaged in these extreme dress-ups. Starting in childhood, I reinvented myself from day to day, dressing and acting differently, but putting on enough of a mask of 'normality' so that no one twigged to my inner turmoil. When I travelled, I could never decide what clothes to take with me as I would never know from one day to the next what I wanted to wear because I was never sure who I was. People around me put my constant changing of clothes down to eclectic tastes—and a large wardrobe.

Jeannie was working as a psychiatric nurse at a Brisbane hospital and recommended a psychiatrist she knew who specialised in treating sexual abuse victims and had even set up a trauma unit at the hospital. I got a referral from my GP; three months later, in May 1997, I had my first consultation with Dr Warwick Middleton. As I later discovered, Dr Middleton, a few years my senior, grew up on a property near Cowra mission. He's a down-to-earth Queenslander with a real big laugh.

One morning I turned up to my appointment looking like Madonna, as in, the pop star; gold creamy satin skirt, which my sister-in-law made me years ago, and white bra top with a cape. Bare midriff.

Dr Middleton looked me over, and asked: 'Who are you today?'

I never 'named' any of my personalities, I told him. 'We're just having a good time.' But it surprised me that he recognised this behaviour; I was used to hiding myself, wearing the mask when I needed to.

And so I embarked on a tumultuous and profound therapeutic journey, hacking through all my 'issues', with trust, falling in love with him, in a healthy textbook case of 'transference'—where a patient redirects to their psychiatrist unconscious feelings, desires and expectations. While I came to trust him very quickly, I still withheld, until relatively recently, details about my intimate life, because I felt awkward discussing my adult sexuality with a man. Maybe I feared he'd think me promiscuous and immoral—a ridiculous fear, I know now.

In that initial period, I spoke to him a lot about my mother. I felt she abandoned me during Wright's case and the attendant ordeal. Actually, I felt abandoned by the whole family and the broader Aboriginal community; no one turned up at court, no one offered me support. Some people didn't know, and weren't told, what Wright had done to me. Others knew but chose to do nothing with the knowledge. And I talked to him freely, to the extent possible at any given moment in time, about the violation I endured as a child.

In time, Dr Middleton diagnosed me with dissociative identity disorder and complex post-traumatic stress disorder, both a legacy of childhood sexual abuse.

Some nights I would drive to the church, and just sit in the car watching the homeless Aboriginals sleeping rough outside. Other times I joined them as they sat smoking on the steps or huddled round a makeshift campfire. At 10 o'clock one night I found myself somewhere in Brisbane. But where was I? I spotted a payphone, stumbled towards it. Pressed the receiver hard against my ear.

'Where are you?' Dr Middleton asked.

'Dunno. It looks like I'm next to Musgrave Park.'

And he talked to me, gently and patiently, talked me back from wherever I had gone, back to the here and now.

'You're okay to go home now,' he said.

This routine went on for years.

***

If you talk about it, you have to kill yourself.

With Dr Middleton's help, I confronted this sinister voice in my head, tracing it back to the paedophile priests who had violated me intermittently in primary school—until, gradually, the voice grew faint, and lost its power over me. Dr Middleton told me repeatedly that he was sure I possessed the strength to overcome my childhood conditioning; that I would never heed the evil message and take my own life.

Two wonderful episodes helped pull me up from a despair that threatened to pull me under for good. The first happened when a psychiatric student of Dr Middleton's observed one of our sessions, obviously with my prior permission. At the start of the session he introduced me to her, though I didn't take much notice. But then at the end of the session, and in front of me, he again said to his student, 'Tjanara is incredibly intelligent ... brave and courageous ... skilled ... One of the smartest women I've ever met.'

This doctor, who I admired and trusted immensely, saw in me these qualities! I felt shock, and deep revelatory contentment. Warwick is still my psychiatrist.

The other incident involved a French man, Marc, who I met three years earlier through Raja Yoga. We were very close; we had this 'karmic' connection, even though he lived in Paris. When I was in a bad way, I'd call him for a chat. And one night I was in a very, very bad way, overwhelmed with darkness. I sent him an email: 'I'm suicidal'.

I woke the next morning to his response.

'As I watched the sun going down last night, I remembered your smiling face.' He called me an empress, and he likewise listed my personal qualities.

I thought: 'Shit, if Marc thinks this about me, it must be true'. And pretty much from that day on, I resolved that my childhood tormentors weren't going to win. I would no longer be the woman who, while on a clothes-buying expedition for her daughter, runs panicked, from the shopping centre, her daughter trailing, panting and confused. That I would transform myself, follow every path to recovery, go back to work, get my degrees. Be a good mother and not a mad one.

That I would never again contemplate killing myself.

14

RECONCILIATION

On my dining table at home, the canvas board is stretched out luxuriously, goading me with its blankness. 'You really reckon you're up to this?' it seemed to be saying. I picked up a paintbrush and dipped it in one of my newly-acquired bottles of acrylic paint.

The brush settled into my hand like a weapon.

This all came about because of an old high school friend, Karen, who ran a community organisation that operated out of the presbytery at St Mary's, the hippy Brisbane church where I spent a lot of time in that period in the late 1990s, as my settlement talks with the Catholic hierarchy dragged on. The organisation worked with Aboriginals, among others, tackling problems such as homelessness and drunkenness, and promoting reconciliation. They were looking for an Aboriginal artist to paint these large canvases with images inspired from the organisation's reconciliation statement.

'Let me do it for you,' I said. 'I'm cheap.' As people who've barely lifted a paint brush before, let alone filled enormous canvases, usually are.

But not long after that afternoon when the empty canvas goaded me, I stood in front of four canvases, each exploding with colour.

One depicted people travelling from disparate places, a cross and a rainbow snake meeting at the centre, and a caption reading, 'We come from all places and all cultures to worship here'. Another traces the bend in the Brisbane River, past Musgrave Park, a traditional ceremonial ground, and St Mary's Church. Yet another explores the three laws of respect, the serpents *Tjuringas*, ceremonial objects, and in the centre, *Baiame*, the sacred spirit. The fourth canvas shows black people and white people holding hands. Some people see in these paintings sperm, a penis and an Uluru-shaped womb.

Not coincidentally, at around this time, I created a dot painting of my own birth—ponds of blue, dots of white, against a flat ochre background. Stars. Light. New beginnings. I gave that artwork to Warwick, and it hangs still in his consulting room. This was my childlike way of saying to him, 'I'm going to be okay'.

To this day I believe that when I paint, I'm channelling the ancestors.

***

I was still heavily embedded in the Catholic scene, with many Catholic friends, including Father Mick Peters in the Townsville diocese, and even some bishops and monsignors climbing the institutional ladder. I guess my Catholic conditioning during childhood and young adulthood was too intense to brush off—it certainly took me a long time to overcome the teachings about sin and guilt, everything that made you feel ashamed of being human. On the other hand, I could also acknowledge the beauty of Catholicism's values, the spirituality and love of God. Like my mother always said, there's plenty of good things about the Church and plenty of bad, so take the good things and leave the rest. But then the Church's hypocrisy about child sex abuse?—this was too tough to reconcile with the 'good' things.

For his part, Bishop Gerry persisted in trying to coax me back to faith, to life as a practising Catholic. Even when he visited the Vatican, around the late 90s, as part of a global delegation that met with the Pope about the child sex abuse crisis, he sent a postcard saying, 'Just thought I'd let you know we're talking about this subject and working hard…'

A confession though: I'm prone to 'past-life' visions (make of them what you will). So after reading the postcard, I saw a vision of myself as an old man in a wheelchair, blanket covering my legs, parked on the veranda at the Vatican. The scene plays out way back in another century. I wear cardinal robes. I'm dying. I just sit there, gazing into the distance and thinking, 'You know, this church isn't what it used to be'.

But for all the visions and residual spirituality, my response to Bishop Gerry's was blunt: 'I'm done with you mob'.

When Ray Wyre, a British expert on sexual crime, visited Australia to talk to bishops and therapists about treatment options for paedophile priests, the Church invited me to his two-day work-shop. I bought Wyre's *The Murder of Childhood*, his chilling book about counselling and investigating brutal sex offenders and serial murderers. He recounts his sessions with Scottish serial killer and paedophile, Robert Black, convicted of the murder of Caroline Hogg, Susan Maxwell and other young girls he abducted, abused and killed in the 1980s. One observation Wyre made at this work-shop stayed with me. When the Catholic abusers were anointed priests, Wyre explained, they viewed themselves as sacred beings who could do no wrong, and this grandiose self-image settled deep in their psyche. In this way they managed to 'split off' the paedophile part of themselves. Because of this delusion about their sacredness, Wyre argued that paedophile priests could never be completely rehabilitated; their self-reckoning could only go so far.

***

During this period in the late 1990s, I focused on my recovery, a journey that culminated—or so I thought—in a meeting that coincided with the end of the millennium. In 1998, I felt well enough to dabble in some work, and took a position as the Indigenous community development coordinator in the mental health unit at Bayside District Health, a job I qualified for, thanks to the counselling course the Church had funded. And Warwick, my psychiatrist, was kindly doubling as a professional mentor, sending me to psychiatric training courses at the University of Queensland, and letting me plunder his impressive library. I read about my condition. I read about psychiatric illnesses generally. I gained Certificates in Mental Health Assessment and others.

Parallel to my developing expertise in mental health, I also took more workshops in Aboriginal women's business and Aboriginal medicine. And through my friend Karen, I met a lapsed Christian Brother who had left the priesthood and married. His wife was a singer, so I hooked up with her and these three other women who all played guitar or other instruments, and we formed a little group. We belted out Celtic, Native American and Aboriginal songs, and we also wrote some of our own, performing at book launches, parties, community events.

I also joined forces with two female dancers—one Aboriginal and a white friend of mine—and called ourselves *Wajin Murri*, meaning 'white woman and *Murri* woman'. We won a government contract to create a song and a play about domestic violence, performing the piece all over Brisbane. At St Mary's, we wrote and performed a work memorialising a military massacre of Aboriginal people in colonial Queensland.

Around this time, I travelled to the US to do a Women's Business healing workshop at St. Catherine's University in Minnesota where I met this old medicine man, a Native American from the Pine Ridge Indian Reservation. He had a PhD in psychology and was a veteran of the Korean war and battles for Indigenous rights. I confessed to him that I was longing to go to Pine Ridge. 'Sure, he said, 'anytime'. And so my friend from the Centre at the University and I got in the car and drove 13 hours to South Dakota. What can I say: my trucking days had habituated me to huge stretches of bitumen, epic road trips springing from spur-of-the-moment decisions.

Which is how I came to experience my first sweat lodge—a small hut decked out with tobacco pouches, a fire pit with hot red stones in the centre—where Native American cleansing ceremonies took place. We all smoked bush sage while the medicine man, his son and grandson played drums. Circling. Singing. Intense heat and smoke. 'Get me out of here,' a voice in my head screamed. And then I saw a flaming gold light carve a path through the pile of hot stones, the stones melting and moulding into the face of a wolf, a hawk flying up from the fire, wings whipping the air, vanishing. I felt a deep sense of awe as if I had been given a sacred gift by them and was being revealed a world of wonder. The transformative effects of this experience lasted for some time after my return to Australia. I knew that I had been through a deeply healing experience and, as he was a medicine man as well as a doctor of psychology, I felt that he and his family had been brought into my life to help me in my recovery.

***

My life slowly filled with discovery, art and a musical joy, but there was one more hurdle to jump. My settlement agreement with the Church left open the possibility of another meeting between me and Leo Wright, with others, including Bishop Gerry, present, on his release from jail; a last step in my healing, I guess. And I wanted to gauge the extent of his remorse, if any.

Shortly after visiting Wright in jail, the only time after he'd been convicted, I followed up with a letter. 'This is your karma.

You should own up to it.' In response, his lawyer warned my lawyer: 'Please tell your client to desist in writing to my client in prison'. So I figured I'd made him feel bad.

Still, on the cusp of the year 2000, Bishop Gerry rang to tell me Wright was out of prison. 'I've checked with Leo,' he explained, 'and it's okay—he's happy to meet with you'.

We designated some neutral building in Brisbane as the venue; so neutral I can't remember which one it was. I had asked the Church to pay for Father Mick Peters to fly down from Townsville, so now he was at my side. I wore an outfit of azure silk from India: kurta top and pants, a flowing shawl. No flesh to be glimpsed. But when I walked through the door of the neutral building, with Mick Peters close behind, Bishop Gerry, who was waiting inside, said, 'You look like Jezebel'.

I froze, winded.

'Are you fucking joking?' I gasped.

What did Bishop Gerry mean by that remark? That I had seduced Wright back then by flaunting my beauty, and now here I was once again, the tormentor of men?

Wright was waiting in the spacious conference room. Beard. Glasses. The regulation white shirt and black pants. Priest-like, only minus the gold crosses. Perhaps a little pudgier than before. But the same smug grin. Earlier, Bishop Gerry told me Wright was bashed in prison. That he was struggling to find work since his release. That the Church did not want to defrock him.

When I approached, he nodded, hello. We all sat around a coffee table.

Bishop Gerry opened the meeting, rather formally. Well, he said, here we were as I requested in the settlement agreement, as part of the reconciliation process. He reiterated that I requested the meeting and Leo agreed to attend. He thanked Mick Peters for coming as my support person.

'Tjanara, say what you need to say.'

I said a lot. Wright listened, his expression impassive.

'And you know what?' I was towards the end of my soliloquy. 'My mother is completely devastated by what you did to me. My mother is unable to even speak about it, it grieves her so much. And she's angry'—I turned to Bishop Gerry—'she's angry at the Church.'

I glowered at Wright.

'I'm very sorry that your mother suffered,' he said.

***

A couple of years after this meeting, the media reported that Wright was working at spiritual retreats as a 'companion' for clients at the Gold Coast Bethel Community Centre, run by the Sisters of St Joseph. The clients included victims of sexual abuse.

***

My job with Bayside District Health proved a stepping stone to a position as an Indigenous social planner in the Queensland Public Service. But when it became apparent that a 'restructuring' of the departmental 'service strategy' was imminent, I thought, 'I'm not in the mood for change'. And then when Arika announced she wanted to do a foundational course at Canberra University, I declared, 'Well you're not going to Canberra without me!' So I replied to an advertisement for an executive Level 1 job in social policy—income support, disability pensions, veteran affairs benefits and so on—in the Department of Prime Minister and Cabinet, and got it. I've always had very good karma with jobs! Within a month, I headed to Canberra for a new chapter.

The department put us up in an apartment while we looked for a house. And that's where we were at about 10.30 on the night of September 11, 2001 when Islamist terrorists turned passenger jets into missiles, hitting the Pentagon and reducing the World Trade Centre to rubble and ash.

John Howard was Prime Minister. The world, including Australia, was about to change, and profoundly.

15

SECRETS AND LIES

A number of realities had failed to sink in the morning I started work at the prime minister's office. First, that my clinching the job was considered a pretty big deal; apparently an Aboriginal employee was a rarity in the department, and sure enough I only came across one other Indigenous person—a woman in the records-keeping section downstairs. Second—and I admit this sounds naive—I didn't fully grasp that the gig would be such bloody hard work.

Then again, I could hardly have picked a more intense and politically explosive moment for my debut in the prime minister's office. In the shell-shocked aftermath of September 11, a day when John Howard, a 'Man of Steel' as US president George W. Bush would admiringly describe him, sheltered in a cellar under the Australian Embassy in Washington, his presence in the US capital a sheer coincidence. And in the wake of the Tampa crisis in August, when the Australian government refused to let more than 400—mainly Afghan asylum seekers, rescued by a Norwegian cargo ship from a distressed Indonesian fishing boat northwest of Christmas Island—set foot on our territorial soil.

And we were in the midst of a divisive and emotional election campaign.

Typically, my 12-hour day started in the office at 7 a.m. with breakfast and the full complement of daily newspapers, laid out for our immediate and urgent consumption. Everyone was on enterprise bargaining agreements, so if you did really well and your supervisor thought you were fantastic you scored a huge bonus at the end of the year. My boss was very smart and very lovely, but she had the whip out. Lunch consisted of a 10-minute dash to pick up a salad roll and rush back to the desk.

I had never written policy documents at such a senior level, never had to turn around huge research at such speed, the pace relentless. Every morning, our papers were scheduled to land in the PM's office by 11 a.m. We researched and wrote in a mad frenzy so that our documents would be ready by 10.30 a.m. at the latest, leaving time for others to sample, proofread, vet, print and deliver up the final product. And Howard insisted on firm specifications for his policy briefings: the document size—no longer than an A4 sheet of paper—the font, the spacing and the borders.

The PM's advisors frequently called me, asking questions or requesting more information and despite the charged environment, my assessment was expected to be frank and fearless, always. The learning curve was so steep, and I was so immersed in the policy detail, so riding on adrenalin, that it took me a while to realise I had considerable rank to pull. On the occasions I needed to approach a line department to ask after a report or obtain information about something the PM wanted, the staff sprung immediately into action.

As you might imagine, we public servants gathered in groups, whispering about the election—as well as for our own jobs. For most of 2001, the government had been on the nose with the electorate, and even though Howard was milking the Tampa crisis for all it was worth politically, a number of us still thought Labor leader Kim Beazley would win.

And then one day, an immigration policy expert on our floor—I'll call him 'Mark'—got shifted into the office next to his boss, displacing an executive who was hastily moved to another room. Mark's new office had a lock on the door, which was seen as vital. Then, in a highly unusual step, a machine that received data cables was moved into his office—ordinarily, we went down to the basement to collect cables. Also unusual: our deputy secretary, Jane Halton, head of the government's people smuggling task-force, was coming down to our floor, all hours of the day and night, locking herself in Mark's office, reading cables with him. And a defence guy who worked up in the international relations and defence policy area descended regularly too, making a beeline for Mark's office. In short, people were coming and going; people who, until now, rarely came and went.

The departmental chiefs told us not to ask Mark or his boss what they were doing behind locked doors. But we worked it out, joining the dots between the flurry of activity in the office and what we read in the media about the developing storm that became known as 'The Children Overboard Affair'. On 6 October, about a month out from the election, a wooden-hulled fishing boat carrying 223 asylum seekers and dubbed 'Suspected Illegal Entry Vessel' (SIEV) 4, was intercepted by *HMAS Adelaide* 100 nautical miles, or 190 kilometres, north of Christmas Island, and then sunk. The next day, Immigration Minister Philip Ruddock said people on the boat had thrown their children overboard and jumped in the ocean after them in a 'disturbing' ploy to secure rescue and passage to Australia. The fact that the adults were wearing life jackets showed their conduct was 'planned and premeditated', the minister said. This claim was repeated by senior government ministers and Howard himself, who remarked, 'I do not want in Australia people who would throw their own children into the sea'.

Within days, the veracity of the government's claim that asylum seekers tossed their children into the sea came under intense scrutiny. By way of 'proof', Defence Minister Peter Reith produced Navy photographs showing asylum-seeker children in the water. In a searing, now famous, radio interview, ABC journalist Virginia Trioli, said to him: 'Mr Reith, there's nothing in this photo that indicates these people either jumped or were thrown?'

One night, after the controversy subsided, we all went out for drinks, Mark included. A co-worker brought up the children overboard scandal.

'What was going on, Mark?' she asked him. 'What were they doing?'

'It's all a fucking lie,' he said. 'Everything they did was a lie and a cover-up.'

The following year, a mainly partisan Senate Select Committee inquiry into what was coyly referred to as 'a certain maritime incident' found that no children were thrown overboard from SIEV 4, that the evidence did not support the allegation and that the photographs purporting to show children thrown into the sea were taken after the vessel sank.

But in 2001, history took its course. Despite its diving popularity for most of that year, the Howard government pulled off an extraordinary comeback and won the election, stoking public fears about immigration, porous borders and the brown-skinned, and mainly Muslim, people who breach them. They demonised vulnerable people—so familiar to us Aboriginals—a strategy that proved to be electoral gold then and since.

Towards the end of the following year, as per our enterprise agreement, I collected a huge bonus, a reward for my punishingly hard work, and bought a house.

As for Mark, he got back his old public-sector job in Tasmania, and left.

***

My public service career progressed sideways, which was fine by me. Still at Prime Minister and Cabinet, I had oversight of a program, run out of the Department of Communications and the Arts, to establish telecommunications and internet for remote communities. Through sitting on the interdepartmental committee, I sussed out that the program's managers were less than thorough in their reporting to us, so I said to my boss, 'Why don't I go and work over there and put a bomb under them?'

I was promptly seconded to the department, and I put the bomb under them.

But from the time I came on board in the PM's department, the Aboriginal policy gurus and executives at ATSIC began urging me to defect.

'What are you doing over *there*. Why would you want to work for Johnny Howard?' they needled.

'I'm just doing my job,' I protested. 'I'm actually trying to help you, to make it easier for you.'

It was true, though, that the intrigue and odious goings on at PM's wore me down. Fortuitously, my boss called me one day, exasperated about ATSIC's financial accountability, or lack thereof.

'ATSIC is not doing anything with their $34 million for the community participation agreements program. Do you know anybody over there?'

My friend, Geoff Richardson, ran ATSIC's National Policy Office, so I asked him if he wanted me to come over and give him a hand. He did. So I applied for a secondment to ATSIC, and got it, of course.

***

Without labouring the details, the next six months or so offered me an illuminating case study into organisational dysfunction. According to law, only ATSIC's Commissioners, on the advice of government bureaucrats, could allocate public funds to this or that program or community. In reality, individual commissioners and officer holders lower down the hierarchy hived off the money as they pleased.

I remember one day a commissioner, who shall remain nameless, charged up to me and my assistant manager, a traditional, and formidable, Warumungu woman called Jackie, demanding $250,000 for a petrol-sniffing prevention program in the town of Yuendumu in the Northern Territory. At the time, we were establishing the procedural framework for 'Community Participation Agreements' under which Aboriginals would work for the dole—a forerunner of more extensive welfare reform that saw government handouts conditional on things like kids attending school. ATSIC had been diverting the money designated for CPAs into other programs; our job was to ensure it stayed put.

'I know you've got a lot of money,' the commissioner barked at us, 'and I want it now'.

'Well you can't have it,' Jackie said, training her gaze on the commissioner.

Righteo, I thought. Let Jackie handle this.

'I've got kids dying from petrol sniffing—'

'You've got to go through proper process. You go to a Commissioners' meeting like everybody else. You put the program up. They tell you if you get the money.'

The Commissioner blustered off, swearing under his breath. We figured someone further up in the hierarchy had told him, 'You can pull money out of CPAs for this or that'.

ATSIC was a place of fraying nerves and infighting, an institution under siege, and in its last throes. Beyond what was merely bad governance, the Commission was also being investigated for financial corruption and embezzlement of funds earmarked for services in remote communities. As a consequence, the Howard government was gradually able to strip ATSIC of fiscal powers, transferring them to the newly-created, independent body, ATSIS—the Aboriginal and Torres Strait Islander Services. In April 2004, the government abolished the Commission altogether, Howard declaring: 'The experiment in elected representation for Indigenous people has been a failure'.

During this terminal phase, an added sting for ATSIC was the nasty odour surrounding its chair, Geoff Clark, who was sued, ultimately successfully, for allegedly taking part in gang rapes in the 1970s and 1980s. On one occasion, I was having coffee in Brisbane with Clark, Michael Mansell, the firebrand Tasmanian activist, and this lawyer who was working at the UN, a white woman. Clark was leering at the poor *migloo*.

'I know you're wearing a thong under there,' he said to her, grinning.

'Shut up, Geoff,' I blasted at him. But he kept up the disgusting harassment.

'Michael,' I turned to Mansell, pleading, 'Take him away'.

Finally, the pair got up and left.

The lawyer was rattled, incredulous.

'What the fuck?' she stammered.

***

Anyway, I thought: ATSIC's on the nose. Get a job somewhere else. And so, I did.

As a lecturer in the Aboriginal Centre at the University of Tasmania, I spent a lovely year over the Bass Strait with Arika, and old and new friends, my Canberra house rented out in the interim—until a white academic soured the gig with constant disparaging remarks about my not having a PhD. I applied for and won the position of Director of the Centre for Indigenous Education at the University of Melbourne, where I fancied I'd hit the professional jackpot—millions to spend, the highly-respected

Justice Susan Crennan, head of the Aboriginal Scholarships Committee, a friendly Deputy Vice-Chancellor, the renowned scholar Professor Marcia Langton in my orbit too—until within a year petty bureaucracy, empire building, in-fighting and damaging innuendo had me off on stress leave, scratching around for new possibilities.

But this is all a prelude to the high-wire drama that came next. Arika told me she wanted to return to full-time uni in Canberra, and said, 'Mum, why don't you find a job there'. I called a former colleague from Prime Minister and Cabinet who now ran the newly-established Office of Indigenous Policy Coordination, soon-to-be shifted into the department of Families, Community Services and Indigenous Affairs under minister, Mal Brough. So, in October 2005, after roughly two years away from Canberra, I returned to the capital and to the public service, as a senior policy advisor.

I did not know, and could not have anticipated, that two years later, as yet another election campaign swung into gear, the lives of Australia's most vulnerable Aboriginals would profoundly change under a radical shift in Indigenous policy—and that I would find myself at the epicentre of the quake. Unwittingly, I had set the scene for the most traumatic and destabilising saga of my professional life, the reverberations palpable to this day.

16

LATELINE AND LIES

As events unfolded during those horrible two years from June 2006 to August 2008, my life was a toxic blizzard of minutiae and detail—endless conferences with lawyers and investigators, wading through documents and writing them, recounting again and again my version of events, the persistent, churning anxiety. Still, little by little I sensed the turmoil engulfing me was just one episode of a much bigger and tragic drama, the last gasp of a government that had been in power more than a decade and was supremely rattled at the prospect of losing it.

That the saga centred on Mutitjulu, the township at the eastern foothills of Uluru, is no surprise: thanks to its proximity to the sacred site, the remote community has a higher than usual profile, an almost symbolic significance. Fame, as we know, does not always bring good things. For a host of reasons, Mutitjulu was, and to a degree, remains a troubled place: as you read on, lest you're inclined to forget, bear in mind no one—least of all me—disputes that depressing reality. I've sometimes wondered if the township's location brings strife of a spiritual kind too, as if in living so close to the rock its inhabitants assume too heavy a burden of responsibility and buckle under the pressure of that mystical, magnetic energy. That energy radiates with almost unbearable intensity at night when the ancestors roam the moonlit rock face.

Before European settlement, Indigenous people visited the rock for ceremonies and seasonal rituals, but they did not live there, not right beside it. I was always told that when people are near Uluru they can no longer run from themselves, they must confront uncomfortable truths and transform their souls.

The rock delivers a painful reckoning to the wicked.

***

At the start of 2006 after a departmental restructure, I worked as an executive Level 2 on Level 3 of Lovett Tower in Woden. My group within the Office of Indigenous Policy Coordination (OIPC) was called the Community Engagement Branch and I was in charge of 'community recovery', exploring policies for tackling domestic violence, sexual abuse, child sexual abuse, trauma and mental problems in dysfunctional Aboriginal communities. My boss was the assistant secretary in the Communities Engagement Branch, a friend called Greg Andrews, newly returned to Canberra.

I knew Greg, who told me he had Indigenous heritage, from my earlier stints in the public service, and even attended his wedding. For the previous 18 months, he was employed by the Northern Territory government running a project called Mutitjulu Working Together, a program aimed at coordinating services between local, territory and federal government agencies. I once visited him in Central Australia during his time there when I was at Melbourne University; we'd discussed professional matters, and I ended up confiding in him about the institutional politics that was getting me down at work.

So, I had no reason to be anything other than optimistic about our future working relationship.

In retrospect, a perfect storm was gathering largely because complex and entrenched problems in remote communities were suddenly attracting media attention. In May, the ABC's *Lateline* program featured an interview with the Crown Prosecutor for Central Australia, Nanette Rogers, on a confidential briefing paper she wrote about sexual violence in Indigenous communities. Originally intended for only a small number of senior police, the paper alleged that Indigenous male culture and the web of kinship helped create a conspiracy of silence around the crimes, which included horrific case studies gleaned from prosecutorial files over the years. Rape. Murder. Incest. Babies too. Perpetrators using traditional law to get off. The background report noted that out of 40 Indigenous communities in Central Australia, only eight had some sort of police presence.

The following night, Mal Brough, the Minister for Indigenous Affairs, appeared on *Lateline* and repeated remarks he had made earlier that day to radio host, John Laws. He criticised negligent Northern Territory authorities. He spoke about dysfunctional Aboriginal communities, though he did not identify any in particular.

'Everybody in those communities knows who runs the paedophile rings,' he told *Lateline* interviewer, Tony Jones.

'You just said something which astonishes me,' Jones said. 'You said, paedophile rings. What evidence is there of that?'

There was 'considerable evidence', Brough insisted. There were 'people at a very senior level' who 'use children at their own whim'.

The next day, the Northern Territory's Labor Chief Minister, Clare Martin, challenged Brough to 'put up or shut up' about his paedophile allegations. The Minister said nothing other than urging journalists not to get fixated on his use of the word 'rings'.

Back in the OIPC, the *Lateline* episode sent everyone into overdrive. Ministerial requests for urgent advice. Brainstorming sessions and conferences. We redoubled on a program for community engagement at a national level, envisaging two-day meetings, a men's meeting, and a women's meeting to discuss sexual violence, domestic violence and substance abuse. I led a team of people dedicated to the task.

And then, on a day when Brough's ministerial advisor came around from Parliament House, I noticed Greg going up and down in the lift to the associate secretary's office, sequestering himself inside with the door closed.

'I've got to keep the door closed,' he explained when I ventured in, needing his signature for something important. 'Because I'm writing this brief for the Minster about going on the *Lateline* program.'

'Why are you doing that? Is the Minister going on *Lateline*?'

No, he explained, *he* was going on *Lateline* to talk about the sexual abuse allegations in remote communities based on what he'd seen on the ground. I should keep this information to myself, he warned. The Minister said he should do so, and he was briefing the Minister about what he'd be saying. They would be coming to his house to film him first thing next week.

'Why? You're a public servant. Let the fucking Minister do it. It's none of your business,' I berated him in my typically indelicate style. 'You're a stupid fool.'

Shortly afterwards I saw an email I was not meant to see, mistakenly forwarded to me from another director who figured it was intended for me all along. It was an email from the Minister's office asking for advice on sending the Army into Aboriginal communities. I went straight to Greg.

'What the fuck is this?' I was incredulous, alarmed. The Minister knew we were planning a national consultation with Indigenous communities, so why on earth were his people investigating extreme measures?

Greg said he would take the issue up with his boss, the head of the OIPC, Wayne Gibbons. Sometime after that Greg told me he was going to Mutitjulu the following month. Perhaps I would like to join him? He knew I knew people out there. A few days before we left for Mutitjulu my friend Jackie, the Warramunga woman from Tennant Creek who I worked with years earlier at ATSIC, told me something curious. She said she had dreamed about me the previous night.

'I thought I'd better come and tell you,' she said. In her dream we were walking in the desert, when all of a sudden, a motorcycle came tearing towards us and knocked me over. The driver of the motorcycle was Greg.

'I want you to be very careful when you go out there,' she insisted, 'because something's going on'.

As to what went on during those four days in Mutitujulu and thereafter, I'm going to give you an edited account, omitting the petty minutiae or details that are highly contested or were ultimately irrelevant in the scheme of things.

On Monday, June 5, we failed to get off the ground at the airport. Too much fog—Canberra sits in a valley that's prone to fog in certain seasons, cutting us off from the rest of the country. Pretty symbolic really. We came back to the airport the next day. On the plane, Greg popped over from his seat in business class—assistant secretaries enjoy a few extra privileges—bringing with him a small box containing Buddhist items. He needed to take the box with him on this trip, he said, showing me the contents. I got the sense from his behaviour over these few months that he'd been traumatised somehow, although he never mentioned anything. He always had essential oils burning in his office and crystals on his desk. It wasn't unusual for him to be showing me something to do with his personal beliefs and practices. But it felt like desperation, like he needed protection. I later talked about this with two people from the community who worked with him closely and learned that there was a reason he would have been that way. He'd violated some business there and I felt like he was protecting himself as best he could. I listened to him but just found it odd that he was sharing it with me on the flight there.

Later, as we were driving to the township, I asked Greg why he was making this trip as he was getting more and more agitated the closer we got to Mutitjulu. He said he was going to have a meeting with the governing council of the Mutitjulu Community Aboriginal Corporation, the body that runs the township, thank them for his time there, and take care of some unfinished business.

And as Greg kept talking, he veered into unsettling topics. He listed complaints about corruption in the Corporation's governing council. He was here to investigate these complaints and was on guard because his enemies would be at the council meeting to intimidate him. Council member, Lesley Calma, was threatening him and his family—he'd notified the NT police, but I should please keep that to myself. There were violent men running grog and *gunja* into the township. His wife was still traumatised from the threats made against their family. And did I know what nickname his former colleagues at the Department of Foreign Affairs and Trade—his CV includes a posting in China—gave him? 'The baby-faced assassin'. He grinned.

And he'd heard rumours that so-and-so—a respected Mutitjulu Elder—was a paedophile.

Well, I thought at this point, I can smell a paedophile a mile away and this man, who I knew well, was not one. This paedophile rumour is not to be confused with the bigger paedophile rumour first alluded to by Brough on *Lateline*—alarming innuendo was being piled onto the justifiable outrage about heinous crimes in Indigenous communities.

Greg asked me to accompany him to Mutitjulu's council meeting, foreshadowing that at this meeting he would deliver the board a stern message from the Federal Government about good governance. In truth—as NT Senator Trish Crossin told Parliament that December, 2006, after much water had flowed under bridge—the community was accustomed to stern messages from the Federal Government, especially since the previous August when the NT Coroner, Greg Cavanagh, investigated the deaths of three petrol sniffers in the township, and while doing so, was assailed by the spectacle of a youth walking into his open-air hearing sniffing petrol from a can.

The following month Gibbons, as OIPC chief, told 12 members of what was then Mutitjulu Community Inc.—the Corporation's predecessor established under NT law—that the Federal Government wanted to see a better return on its investment. If Mutitjulu wanted to continue receiving federal money, Gibbons warned, it would need to change its constitution, including reserving half its council seats for women and incorporating under a federal act that would bring the governing body under the regulatory authority of the Registrar of Aboriginal Corporations. Gibbons said he had been given $3 million to invest in the central desert Ngaanyatjarra Pitjantjatjara Yankunytjatjara Lands for petrol-sniffing diversion—but the money couldn't be delivered under the existing structure. Greg, who was also at that September (2005) meeting, similarly urged the community to make the change: their current set-up under NT law was okay for sporting clubs, he argued, but for Mutitjulu it was a bit like using a Mazda 121 on bush roads when what they needed was a four-wheel drive.

While largely aware of this backstory, I was nonetheless shocked by what I perceived as Greg's strident and unnecessarily provocative tone at the council meeting. After honouring the traditional owners, he told the councillors that he was delivering a message directly from Brough. Again, he reminded them that the Commonwealth delivered two-thirds of the community's funding. He said the Government remained concerned about conditions at Mutitjulu, warning that if the Corporation wasn't careful, the government would be sending in an administrator and the community would lose control of their funds, including the 'gate money' collected from entry fees to the national park. The Government did not want Mutitjulu to become 'like Wadeye'[4].

The mood soured fast. Mario Giuseppe, a community health worker, lashed out at Greg, asking how he dared to come back as a government man and turn on the community. 'Don't come here talking with your forked tongue,' Mario railed. I looked down at the floor, embarrassed, thinking, 'Greg, you're a fuckwit. This is not how you talk to Aboriginal people.'

But it was the meeting the next day in the lounge room of a Mutitjulu youth worker, Rahm Adamedes, which changed the course of my career and much more besides. Again, Greg asked that I accompany him because he needed 'a witness'.

Adamedes' company had a contract with the community to run a juvenile diversionary program involving what was then called 'new media'—video and audio, utilising cameras and other software to produce music videos, games, etc. He worked alongside Mutitjulu's sport and recreation officer, Michael Presley, who was there, too, seated on the couch. Adamedes expressed his concerns about what he regarded as financial mismanagement and corruption in the community's affairs. Funds earmarked for school holiday programs, sports weekends and other projects were being diverted for other purposes, he said. He made various claims against various council members, but for present purposes only one was critical: he accused Dorothea Randall, who worked

---

4   Wadeye—the Aboriginal community at Port Keats had been in the news because of rioting by gangs of young men; and the Minister went there earlier that year to tell the community that all their Centrelink welfare payments would be cut off if they didn't get their act together.

as a bookkeeper for the Mutitjulu council, of paying substantive amounts of money to her family members to run youth activities.

He was talking about the same Dorothea I had met when I was 21, the daughter of Uncle Bob Randall, who for decades had been my culturally adopted sister. My immediate response on hearing the allegations was to blurt, 'I've known Dorothea Randall for over 25 years!'

The allegations sounded convoluted, tangential to my professional brief and small fry. I just wanted to get out of there and get on with my women's work. I did not know these two men, so couldn't judge their credibility. At best Rahm seemed yet another well-intentioned *migloo* with grandiose ideas who believed that within a few months he could fix an ailing community where others had laboured for decades and failed. In the seemingly endless departmental interrogations that came to pass in the following months, I was upfront about my underwhelming response to the allegations raised in this meeting. Sometimes my bluntness and honesty are a curse—these admissions were interpreted as evidence of a blasé and apathetic approach to problems in Indigenous communities, inappropriate for a public servant.

Incidentally, I later discovered that Michael, the sports officer, was also related to Dorothea through his wife—a status he came to see as insurance against being run out of town.

But at this juncture in the meeting, Adamedes said he wanted to show Greg something on the computer in another other room. Michael and I stayed seated in the lounge room, not speaking. Greg and Rahm returned. Greg requested us all to keep the meeting confidential. I replied that of course I would do that. Greg repeated his instruction the next day: I was allowed to speak to Dorothea, he clarified, and listen to her side of the story. The OIPC needed all the facts, but I wasn't to divulge any information from our meeting with the youth workers.

On Wednesday, I proposed to Greg that I stay an extra day at Mutitjulu for a more extensive meeting with the women—Dorothea had told me they were keen to discuss some difficult issues. Greg agreed. I made arrangements to meet him and Louise Atherton, the new project coordinator of the Working Together Project, at Yulara airport to return his hire car and pick up my new one. When they arrived, I took the opportunity to counsel Greg against taking sides in Mutitjulu, advising him to tone down his anger against certain individuals, his constant references to his past 'trauma' in the community and above all, to refrain from propagating gossip about the alleged paedophile—people were starting to talk, I warned him. He gave a mumbled response that he'd been thinking the same thing himself.

He flew back to Alice Springs where he was to spend the night before returning to Canberra the next day.

It was Thursday morning and two days after flying out of Canberra, when all hell broke loose. I had gone to meet Dorothea at the council offices and was momentarily seated at her desk when her phone rang. She handed it to me. At the end of the line was a very upset and angry Adamedes. I had breached his confidence from Tuesday's meeting, he said. I had told people about his claims against Dorothea and others, and now people were out to get him.

'Listen to me,' I said. 'Don't be disrespectful to me as an Indigenous woman. Are you *Murri*? Are you *Migloo*?' I felt that he was telling me what to do, because he presumed to know these people better than anyone including me. I'd known them for 30 years; he'd been there for only about 18 months. In addition, I'd heard from various community members that they had issues with him in his role as community youth worker. I suggested we discuss his issues over a cup of tea next day at the Cultural Centre at Uluru.

Shortly afterwards I was in a meeting with the Mutitjulu's CEO, Myra Spurling, discussing government programs, funding gaps and the community's needs, when Greg phoned me. He said he'd received an email from his boss, Gibbons, and a phone call from Adamedes, relating to allegations I had leaked confidential information from the meeting with the youth workers. Suffice to say the conversation was less than constructive. I felt he was accusing me without evidence. He later denied he was accusing me at all, insisting he was simply telling me what he'd heard. I gave him a rundown on every person I'd spoken with, every issue I'd dealt with, since Tuesday—governance training, domestic abuse, restraining orders...

A short time later, he rang again—he was in the Qantas Club in Alice Springs, waiting for his flight to Canberra. I was to leave Mutitjulu immediately, he ordered. For my own safety. I pleaded with him: I had a women's meeting arranged for that afternoon. He told me I was not to go to it. That I should meet with Adamedes, smooth things over with him, and then I was to head to Yulara, the township near Uluru, and not return to Mutitjulu. His order to vacate was about 'risk management', he said. How was I at risk? No one was threatening me. But I did what I was told—what else could I do? I told Dorothea the women's meeting wouldn't go ahead, and returned to Yulara shortly after.

On Friday morning I spent an hour and a half with Adamedes at the Cultural Centre there. He rambled, agitated. He broke down crying, and again, accused me of breaking confidence. I denied the accusation, telling him that I did not know who leaked the information. Maybe Michael did, who knows? I explained I had a cultural connection to the Randall family stretching back 25 years. But it was hard to get a word in amid his torrent of words.

Finally, I snapped. He was a young *migloo*, and I said, 'This is not your country'. The comment sounds harsher than I intended;

Aboriginals use this rebuke against each other frequently, designating rights by reference to clan and traditional lands.

'I have a responsibility to these people and to this area,' I continued.

'Are you acting as a Government officer or are you acting on your cultural obligations?' he retorted.

There's no conflict between my cultural responsibilities and my professional obligations, I assured him. Eventually, he calmed down and thanked me for listening to him. But when I flew back to Canberra that afternoon it was with a sense of utter foreboding.

A fitful sleepless weekend followed. By Monday I decided on proactive damage control, so I called our Group Manager, Helen Hambling. She agreed to meet me for coffee even though it was the Queen's Birthday long weekend. I recounted the traumatic events of the previous week. We should develop guidelines on engaging with Indigenous communities, base them on mutual regard and respect, I suggested.

On my return to the office on Tuesday, it was patently obvious I was in the deep freeze. Greg passed me in the corridors without acknowledgment. The emails emanating from his office had neither greeting nor signature—no 'Tj' or 'Owl', my totem, no 'GA' or emoji. Searching through my backlog of emails, I came across one headed; 'CONFIDENTIAL: Child Abuse and neglect & Mutitjulu dysfunction'. The email, from Greg to chief Gibbons, had been forwarded to me on June 5, just prior to our leaving for Mutitjulu, but I'd missed it then. Among other things, Greg tells Gibbons that his talks with community stakeholders in Mutitjulu suggest the situation is 'grim' as it would appear that 'alcohol, marijuana, and petrol consumption, child neglect, intimidation, violence, corruption and mismanagement have escalated. There is also a risk that the current CEO is burnt out and not able to stand up against the bullies.' Finally, he'd learned 'Mr Calma'—a reference to Graham Calma, Lesley's brother—was still working in publicly-funded positions in the community, and was deputy chair of the Uluru-Kata Tjuta National Park board, despite a criminal record, which he, Greg, was endeavouring to obtain.

Interesting, I thought. I sent on the memo to my personal email address.

After 5 p.m., Greg came into my office. He reiterated that he'd ordered me out of Mutitjulu because he was doing 'risk management'. I asked him if, in delivering the sharp message to the Mutitjulu community, he was under instructions from Gibbons. Yes, he was, he said. Terse.

Unable to stop the churning in my stomach, I rushed to my doctor's and obtained a certificate for three weeks' sick leave.

The following Wednesday, June 21, I sat around a conference table with Greg and Helen Hambling. He criticised me for attending a leadership forum that morning without getting his permission first. I explained I had only learnt about the forum that same morning, had tried unsuccessfully to contact him, and had asked a colleague to inform him of my whereabouts. He again brought up the allegation that I leaked 'confidential information' to people in the Mutitjulu community and 'unnamed' others. I again denied the accusation. I told him Dorothea Randall had told me she'd contacted him on the Friday of our week in Mutitjulu and denied I'd leaked any details of the meeting with Adamedes or that she'd ever suggested otherwise. She said Adamedes' claims against her were well-known in the community—he even raised them in a council meeting as far back as January—and in a community of a few hundred people, the very idea of 'confidentiality' is a joke: everyone knew everyone else's business.

Anyway, if you want an objective view of how this discussion unravelled, some months later, Hambling remarked to an investigator that she had been 'surprised and dismayed at the breakdown in the relationship' between Greg and me, 'which quickly became evident'. At the meeting's end I had pleaded: 'You have to trust me, Greg, if we are to work together'.

But dread was seeping into my bones. I went home. And then, at 10.30 that night, I turned on *Lateline,* not knowing the report I was about to watch would trigger an earthquake.

Centring on Mutitjulu, the report ventilated horrific claims of child sex abuse and bureaucratic inaction from credible sources. But especially alarming was the anonymous contribution of someone the program described as a 'former youth worker'. This man cried as he repeated Minister Brough's more sensational claims about paedophile rings in the township, adding a few of his own.

'The people who are in control are the drug dealers and the petrol warlords and the paedophiles,' he said. 'I saw women coming to meetings with broken arms, or with screwdrivers or other implements through their legs.'

And in answer to another question: 'It's true that there are predatory men in the Central Deserts who are systematically abusing young children. I've been told by a number of people, of men in the region who go to other communities and get young girls and bring them back to their community and keep them there as sex slaves...'

Sex slaves.

All the incidents of sexual abuse and violence that he saw, he reported to the police, he said. But violent threats against him and his wife, threatening phone calls even as they were in hospital with the birth of their child, forced him to withdraw his statements.

'And is that your biggest regret?' the *Lateline* journalist asked.

'It's something that I've been thinking about a lot.'

His face was concealed in shadow, his voice digitised. Still, peering into the set I had no doubt; the outline of his shape, the surrounding context, his hat, his jumper, was more than enough for the spark of recognition. He was no 'youth worker', former or otherwise. The man backing the Minister's assertions about petrol warlords and paedophile rings at Mutitjulu was his senior bureaucratic advisor on Aboriginals in central Australia: Greg Andrews.

The morning after the *Lateline* report, Northern Territory Chief Minister, Clare Martin, announced her government would hold a major inquiry into violence against children in Aboriginal communities.

Let's be clear: contrary to the accusations, I did not leak details of the meeting with Adamedes in Mutitjulu to Dorothea Randall. But after this *Lateline* episode, sensing something rotten afoot in government policy on Indigenous affairs, and realising I would be shafted at work in any event, I leaked. A lot.

I called Amy McQuire, an Aboriginal journalist who had crashed at my place at an earlier time and who worked for Chris Graham at the *National Indigenous Times*.

'I think they're going to do something to me,' I told her. I said I had a story for Chris and (journalist) Brian Johnstone.

The three journalists, Chris, Brian and Amy, came to my house. I told them everything: what I knew, what had been done to me, what the Minister had done, what Greg had done. I told them who the 'former youth worker' really was. When we were done I was given a 40-page transcript of my interview, which I placed in the coffee table drawer.

At the end of the month I lodged an harassment claim against Greg Andrews. An investigator was called in to compile a report. The claim failed. In his defence, Greg raised a laundry list of concerns about my character and performance. That on the plane to Central Australia I had told him some Indigenous people in the OIPC were upset because they perceived him as supporting the Australian Government agenda and not theirs—but a public servant was obliged to rise above race politics, Greg argued. That on this flight I had also disobeyed a seat belts' sign—which, in retrospect he interpreted as a symptom of my increasingly erratic conduct and poor judgment. That I had had conflicts with another manager in the public service and in my past job at Melbourne University. That my interest in spirituality and healing was interfering with my work. That while in Mutitjulu, I had neglected to answer his calls. (My mobile was out of battery one evening.) That during a private visit of mine to Tasmania, I had rubbed a few Indigenous academics the wrong way and met with Michael Mansell, a radical black activist and vociferous critic of the federal government. (Michael is an old mate.) He even cited a two-line email I had sent him a week earlier after I had learnt that his young son was having an operation, as refuting my claim of feeling harassed and intimidated.

'I did not know he (Greg's son) was unwell,' I wrote to Greg in the email. I signed off with 'sending love and light', to him, his wife and his son.

Greg surmised that to some degree my complaint was motivated by his rejection of my view that as a senior Indigenous female, he should be subservient to me. (A crude overstatement.) He saw an element of my grievance as 'payback'.

This was but one instalment in my comprehensive character assassination; stay tuned for more.

Among the character references Greg compiled for the investigator was an observation by the NT coroner, hearing the previous year's inquest into the deaths of two young petrol sniffers in Mutitjulu, at which he appeared.

'I have rarely,' the coroner remarked, 'met a more qualified, committed and culturally supportive advisor in terms of Aboriginal substance abuse problems than Mr Andrews. His work is simply outstanding.'

Again, my tribulations were a microcosm of a broader conflagration. At the start of July, the Federal Government froze funding to the Mutitjulu Corporation and appointed an administrator to that body. In its reasons for the latter, the Registrar of Aboriginal Corporations stated that the department had 'lost confidence' in the Corporation and its governing committee. The committee immediately challenged the decision in the Federal Court. (They were ultimately successful.)

After my revelations, the *National Indigenous Times* shifted into gear, unleashing their banked-up arsenal of stories one at a time. They outed Greg Andrews as *Lateline*'s anonymous 'former youth worker', after which numerous media outlets referred to him as 'the fake youth worker'. Then four days later, a story with the headline, 'OIPC boss promised criminal records by senior staffer, leaked emails reveals', reported the substance of the confidential email from Greg to Gibbons on the morning of our departure to Mutitjulu.

And on it went as the *NIT* went sniffing through Greg's profile. Back in April he 'grossly misled' a federal Senate Inquiry into Petrol Sniffing in remote Aboriginal communities. He told parliament that he lived in Mutitjulu for nine months, when actually he lived 20 kilometres away, at the five-star Ayers Rock Resort.

He claimed that in Mutitjulu, 'young people were hanging themselves off the church steeple on Sunday and their mothers were having to cut them down', although his evidence revealed he only witnessed one such incident, and police said they had no record of it. He subsequently apologised in writing to the Senate, acknowledging he'd never lived in Mutitjulu and that he 'inadvertently misled' parliament, including about the findings of the coronial inquiry into the petrol sniffing deaths.

In the days that followed, from my home computer, I parcelled vital intelligence to Dorothea at the coalface, sending her

a handful of work emails Greg had circulated to various colleagues, including me. One suggested that programs to curb
petrol sniffing were failing and alcohol bans regularly breached.
Another—'Postscript to the Mutitjulu substance abuse action
plan'—advised Gibbons that the NT government 'is perhaps
not living up to its side of the bargain' on policing in Mutitjulu,
and relayed Greg's concerns about the new project manager 'who
appears focused towards the community as a client at the expense
of the Australian Government'.

Greg commented that the project manager had told him,
'I [Greg] had left "a few people in Mutitjulu nursing wounds"—
these are presumably the drug dealers and corrupt individuals,
whose activities she appears to be unaware of'. Another memo
from Greg to Gibbons marked 'Confidential: FWL Sexual health
screening', revealed the Government was considering screening
young Mutitjulu children for signs of sexual abuse.

So I guess I should not have been surprised by what happened
next. On Friday, July 21, I was at work where I had moved to
a different branch, a band-aid measure pending the outcome of
my claim against Greg, when, just before 2 p.m. my mobile rang.
At the other end was a very alarmed Arika.

'The police are here. They're raiding the house.'

17

INDICTED

As Arika waited at the end of the line, I immediately pictured the 40-page transcript of my interview with *NIT*, sitting in the coffee table drawer. Whispering into my mobile, I told her about the document and its whereabouts.

'If you can get that thing out of there and hide it somewhere without them seeing, that would be a good thing to do, darling.'

It was 10 minutes to four in the afternoon by the time I pulled up outside our house at 9 Colbeck Street, Mawson. At the door, an Australian Federal Police officer handed me a document headed 'Rights of the Occupier' together with a copy of the warrant, issued under the *Crimes Act 1914* and bearing what seemed to me a long list of names, 16 in all—the journos at *NIT*, Dorothea and Uncle Bob, other community leaders at Mutitjulu, Greg Andrews, Wayne Gibbons. The authorities sought information relating to all these people.

I rang the only lawyer in my contact book, Sydney's George Newhouse, a long-time advocate for Indigenous and other marginalised groups.

'What do I do about a warrant? There's police here.'

'Read it to me,' Newhouse said.

'...originals or copies of: diaries, telephone records, email addresses, business and private addresses, notes, service provider account details, letters, emails, facsimiles, business records, computer hardware and software, discs and CDs, media records, newspapers and electronic records...'

Meanwhile, I watched the AFP officers comb my study. From the top shelf of a side cupboard, they bagged two Optus documents. From the bookshelf, three print-outs, including one regarding the inquiry into petrol sniffing in remote Aboriginal communities, and an email from Greg. From the wastepaper basket under my desk, a hard copy of an email I had sent from my work address to my Optus account. From a tray on the shelf next to my desk, my diary with an Aboriginal motif on the front. They seized my Dell computer hard drive and my laptop. They took photographs and videos. They recorded audio of our interactions.

But my ancestors were smiling on me that day: they did not find the 40-page interview transcript.

Being raided by the AFP is one avenue to instant stardom. The next day my new boss phoned me, incredulous.

'Tjanara, your lawyer is on the news saying all this stuff. What's going on?'

Newhouse, was indeed all over the news, describing the raid on my home as part of a campaign against Australia's Indigenous community and describing me—wrongly—as a member of the Mutitjulu community, which the *Queensland Times* noted 'has been at the centre of a series of stories published in the *National Indigenous Times* over the past two weeks'.

He declared: 'This is a campaign of fear and intimidation that the government is launching against a defenceless Aboriginal community'. To which the *NIT* reported, on the same day, an additional statement attributed to me: 'Let me assure the government that this issue is not going away and that we've not yet got to the bottom of the government's skullduggery'.

All these reports proved detrimental to my position in the public service and, at the time, while I made futile attempts to distance myself from them, the horse, needless to say, was bolting.

On Sunday, a call from my employer, from someone in the Stalinist-sounding, 'People Branch'. I was suspended with pay for breaching the public service Code of Conduct.

On Tuesday I sent a group email to my contacts.

Hello everyone,

The AFP issued a search warrant on my house on Friday, and I was suspended from day job at OIPC on Sunday. Wanted to let our network know. Happy for your support, verbally or in your thoughts.

Support came from *Sydney Morning Herald* columnist, Alan Ramsey, who weighed in on my behalf the following weekend with a scorching critique of the police raid, the Federal Government's Indigenous policies, and the ABC for the 'fake youth worker' controversy. The OIPC, he wrote, is the 'white-run successor to the black-run ATSIC, the Hawke government's Aboriginal and Torres Strait Islander Commission, which the Howard Government spent nine years slowly garrotting… Tjanara Goreng is not a terrorist,' Ramsey argued. 'She is a bureaucrat. She also has Indigenous heritage.'

*** *

'This is a tape recording of Ms Tjanara Goreng Goreng being accompanied by Angela Palombi of the Investigative Services Branch, OIPC, and Colin Greef of Active Services, OIPC, to Office 3 of 21A, Level 3, Lovett Tower, Woden, ACT, for her to collect her personal belongings. The tape will be running during the collection of the items…'

Ms Palombi: Okay. Tjanara, do you agree that the time now is 5.40?

Me: Looks like it.

Ms Palombi: On Wednesday, 26 July 2006?'

Me: Mm.

Ms Palombi: Tjanara, do you agree that Colin and I accompanied you into your office 3 of 21A, Level 3, Lovett Tower, Woden—

Me: I guess you did.

Ms Palombi: —ACT—

Me: I'd say it is.

…

Me: These books are mine, so go ahead and have a look at them.

Ms Palombi: Sure. Well, I'll wait for you, then perhaps we can do it together.

Me: …I'll get you to do that. This is exciting. I've never done this before. You can look through that. That's my … that I usually write work in.

…

Me: Somebody's been in here. My remote access little doovey thing goes in here, was sitting here.

…

Me: You can check the back of this painting, that it belongs to me.

***

A letter from the Group Manager from Corporate Support elaborated on the reasons for my suspension. It cited the recent statements from Newhouse, 'said to be made on your behalf', in particular statements about the Government's approach and actions in Mutitjulu. I also failed to disclose a conflict of interest, namely that I was, in Newhouse's words, 'a member of the Mutitjulu community'. Finally, the letter noted, there is information suggesting my involvement in the release of confidential information, information sufficiently compelling to authorise an AFP search warrant. That issue is now in the hands of the AFP.

I sought a review of my suspension, what else could I do? I denied the 'alleged inappropriate release of confidential information to parties not authorised to receive this information'. I explained that I was not a member of the Uluru/Mutitjulu community, but possessed a strong spiritual and cultural connection to the place, not easily understood through a European frame of reference.

'My cultural connection is through my great-grandfather's law,' I wrote in my defence. 'Our Songline, which connects our *Tjukurpa* traverses Uluru, 'and in my sacred and secret cultural ceremonial traditions I was introduced to the sacred meaning of this...' As for my long and close bond with the Randalls, I knew them in Canberra and when they returned to Mutitjulu in 2004, I visited them. Yes, I was culturally adopted by this family who are the traditional custodians of Uluru and the surrounding lands, but this only confers on me a right to study and learn with Elders, with my grandmother, 'Nanna' Barbara Nipper.

As my review progressed, the file against me grew fatter, with 'Corporate Support' finding more facts worthy of concern. That in February—long before the trouble started—I posted three items to the online discussion forum of *The Australian*. The first, signed with my name and position in the OIPC and headed, 'Leaders bashing public servants in Indigenous Affairs' was actually an impassioned defence of the OIPC's work. The second and third, both written in my personal capacity, opined on Aboriginal identity ('Who wants to be an Aborigine?') and on Islamic fundamentalism ('Muslims overreacting').

That also in February, I solicited contact with journalist, Patricia Karvelis, of *The Australian*. Not so—she initiated contact with me, and I rebuffed her overtures. That again in February, I invited Warren Snowdon MP, Labor's Shadow Parliamentary Secretary for Indigenous Affairs, to 'get in touch and perhaps catch up for a coffee sometime' despite it being improper for a public servant to have unauthorised contact with someone from the Opposition front bench. Warren is an old mate and veteran of Aboriginal politics, who I first met in Canberra in 1983. I was open about my meeting with him at Parliament House, and on my return, even told my bosses about the substance of our conversation.

At one point, the Branch Manager of Indigenous Programs Investigations, referred to advice from the AFP that I have, 'under various names, a criminal history'. While this was news to me, I was assured the allegation would not be given weight in the review.

In November, a week before the Federal Court was to hear the community's challenge to the government's appointment of an administrator to the Mutitjulu Corporation, the AFP raided Dorothea's home and offices in the township. The warrant sought documents relating to Greg Andrews, among others.

'Why aren't all Australians entitled to know,' George Newhouse told *Crikey*, once again in the limelight as the community's lawyer, 'that senior public servants have misled the Senate, assumed false identities and slandered the Mutitjulu community on national television or that they have manipulated the community so that they could strip their self-government?'

And not only *that* community. By the following June the entire mosaic came into sharp relief. On the 15th of that month, the NT government released the report of the inquiry triggered by the 'fake youth worker' *Lateline* report—called *Little Children are Sacred*. The document ran to more than 300 pages and contained 91 recommendations. Much of the report's content was not new; Aboriginal researchers and activists had been writing about endemic social dysfunction in their communities for many years, mostly in vain.

But six days later—virtually a year to the day of the infamous *Lateline* report and precisely a year since the AFP raid on my home—the Howard Government, on the eve of a federal election campaign and purportedly in response to *Little Children are Sacred*, announced the radical Northern Territory Emergency Response, now known as 'the intervention'. The Commonwealth had to act, the Prime Minister, said, because the NT government was taking too long to respond to its own report.

There would be a substantial deployment of police to remote communities; medical teams for child health checks; a massive roll-out of new housing; widespread alcohol and pornography bans. Despite the NT Aboriginal Land Rights Act 1975 which had enabled many Traditional Owner groups to claim back their lands in the NT, the Federal government wanted to bring in compulsory five-year land leases on Aboriginal lands and they needed the agreement of those communities who had had their lands returned to them.[5] Other measures included the suspension of the permit system in Indigenous lands, the suspension of the

---

5   In his film Utopia, John Pilger discusses Aboriginal community suspicions that the Federal government was going to grant mining leases over some of these lands, as they had seen mining exploratory helicopters over lands in the NT from 2005 through to 2010. So, there was a lot of talk that the government was using this legislation as a way to get traditional owners to agree to lease back lands in exchange for basic funding for utilities such as housing, water, sewerage etc. in those remote communities put under the NT Emergency Response law.

Racial Discrimination Act in the NT. Prior to this, Aboriginal people had been winning land rights claims across the territory since the introduction of the Aboriginal Land Rights Act in 1975 and a large percentage of Northern Territory land had been returned to Aboriginal communities. Welfare payments would be quarantined onto a 'basics card' for essential items. The army would provide logistical support to the government effort—hence, the email I saw more than a year ago about sending in the military to remote communities.

And the community at the frontline of this emergency response? Well, the community at the foothills of Australia's most iconic tourist attraction, the traditional custodians of Uluru, the beleaguered, intensely scrutinised township of Mutitjulu.

I don't need to tell you how incensed I felt; vindicated but incensed. What right did they have to send the army into poor Aboriginal communities? How was bashing poverty-stricken townships that lacked for jobs or local businesses going to help anyone? This is not me denying the scale of the crisis in Aboriginal Australia, but some of us were working on solutions furiously—durable solutions: bilateral agreements with the states; Aboriginal communities themselves deciding priorities, be it the training of health and social workers or the funding of local organisations. Why would you not consult the communities in question? Why paint all Aboriginal men as alcoholics, pornographers, paedophiles? Why run the bulldozer over people, issue orders from an ivory tower in Canberra?

The intervention felt like another colonial invasion, another rounding up of blacks.

Of course, I had my own, more personal reasons for despair—in limbo, waiting to be charged, attending countless meetings with lawyers, a cloud over my name. After the AFP raid, my rental home in Mawson felt tainted, violated. We moved into a new rental house in Queanbeyan. The public servants at the OIPC were warned not to talk to me unless they wanted to implicate themselves in wrongdoing. So, all my Aboriginal friends abandoned me and disappeared; nobody came to my forty-ninth birthday party. The only person who stayed in touch with me was Geoff Richardson, my friend from ATSIC who said, bless him, 'They can fuckin' raid my house, I'll give them what for!'

Every week I saw the mental health worker at Queanbeyan Hospital. I was near suicidal.

On 29 October 2007, the ACT Magistrates Court committed me to stand trial in the Supreme Court on seven charges of disclosing information that came into my possession as a Commonwealth public servant, and which I had a duty not to disclose, contrary to section 70 (1) of the Crimes Act 1914. Leaking details of the meeting with Rahm Adamedes to Dorothea. Leaking four internal emails, including ones relating to sexual health screening, petrol sniffing and governance problems at Mutitjulu.

Another count related to an email that I forwarded to Arika in March with the covering note, 'You might be interested in these documents on self-determination for your essay'. The email, which had been circulating at work, related to a United Nations working group for the Draft Declaration on the Rights of Indigenous People. Two documents attached to the email were in the public domain, and those were the ones I thought might come in handy for Arika's uni essay. I didn't realise there was a third internal working document also attached, originating from DFAT and titled 'Draft talking points for Ottawa, Moscow and London', which, as the title suggests, foreshadowed scheduled discussions with Canada, Russia and the UK about the Draft Declaration. Arika did not even open the email, that's how enticing the subject matter was for a 21-year-old. Still, this truly unconscious transgression on my part was added to the list of charges, each one carrying a maximum penalty of two years.

I pleaded 'not guilty' on all counts.

I was staring at the prospect of 14 years' jail.

By now you'll believe me when I say that I never stay in the pit for very long. I saw a job advertisement for a senior lecturer at Southern Cross University's Lismore campus in New South Wales. The position involved working with trauma expert, Judy Atkinson, around sexual abuse in Indigenous communities. Figuring it would take at least a year before my case ran, and knowing my career as a Commonwealth public servant was dead in the water, I applied for the job, got it and blew out of Canberra.

18

BAD SPIRITS

In the isolated coastal community of Kalumburu, 900 kilometres northeast of Broome at the tip of Western Australia, the Indigenous Elder ladies kept their homes perfectly clean. The missionaries had taught them about domestic standards all right. An Elder led me through her house; no refrigerator, a broken foam mattress, but, still immaculately tidy. Unsurprisingly, the missionaries—the community started its life in the early years of the 20th century as a Benedictine mission—also drummed a few other habits into the Indigenous locals; and so when the mission bell tolled at 5 o'clock every afternoon, these same women headed faithfully to church where a rather rancid-looking old priest waited for them.

Despite its church bells and devout old ladies, Kalumburu was a vision of dystopia. In mid-2007, 16 Aboriginal men, including community leaders, were charged with 103 sexual assault offences, such as molesting young children and exchanging cigarettes for sex with underage girls. One woman I met was nearly killed by her husband after he raped and bashed her when she was pregnant. She was desperate to get out of there.

The WA magistrate, Sue Gordon, called up Judy, my boss at Southern Cross, and asked her if she could establish a community-based recovery program for the township. Now Judy had asked me to keep running what she'd started; so every three months I spent three weeks there as a project manager and facilitator, working alongside a handful of newly-minted trauma specialists, community development workers and student researchers. It was my job to evaluate the programs, do the research, collect the statistics and manage the finances.

I guess it was one way to get a swift sense of perspective, working with the women. Few people owned cars, so the community loaned us a bus and we drove the old ladies and the young ones into the bush. Everyone would fish at the mouth of the river, and as they did so, the stories dribbled out, some stories from very long ago. One Elder was a child survivor of the Forest River massacre—a massacre, I soon learnt, in the Kimberley region in 1926. At the time a state royal commission concluded two policemen killed 11 Aboriginals.

Taking me on a walking tour of the town one day, an older lady stopped in front of a typically dilapidated house.

'That's the house where they do the filming,' she said.

She was talking about the men who made pornography. All day long this violent rap music blared from inside the place. It was an awful, awful place. We encouraged the young girls involved to paint or draw and talk about their experiences. None of them were going to school. They told us they were forced to engage in pornography. They cried.

Our program was based around the tradition, *Dadirri*, where we listen deeply to each other, and conclude with a smoking ceremony, for cleansing. A few days after one of these sessions, the girls came back, feeling different, more positive.

'Well you've told us a story,' we said to them. 'Now tell us another story: how we might change things.' And we made artwork, took notes, made maps; took stock of the resources that already existed in the community, and considered what resources the government might provide to help that change come about.

And then I started doing cultural things with the kids: dancing and singing and playing sticks, until pretty soon the grandparents joined in. They said, 'Oh, we haven't done this since we were little kids.' Another time, an independent group of filmmakers were travelling through Kalumburu filming travel documentaries from Darwin to Broome. When they stopped in Kalumburu they found out what we were doing, and asked if they could make a film of our work. We agreed.

An old white-haired man in a wheelchair had been among the first lot of children housed in the dormitories which the Benedictine mission built. He was among the first children sexually abused by the priests who found it all too easy to prey on them while their parents lived in rusty iron sheds out in the bush. After all the kids were snatched and herded into the dormitories, the priests tied up the fathers and beat them into submission.

Once we heard these stories, it became apparent that we weren't just dealing with today's violent predators, but with complex generational abuse. So, we helped the community devise a program to clear the air about these past horrors, too—a women's group congregated under the mango trees, and the men congregated separately, guided by one of the young community development workers, who also had trauma training.

After about 8 months, there was a big fight in this one family. Some of the men wanted to go down to the men's group; the other relatives wanted them to stay put and not get involved. Fists flew in the middle of the street. And then the old man in the wheelchair, the man who was abused by the priests, appeared on the scene and yelled at the young men obstructing the others.

'This is important,' he said. 'We have to do it. You have to let them do it.'

The fists dropped, an uneasy calm descended. Eventually that family got involved in the men's group, which marked a turning point in our healing work. Gradually more and more people started coming to the group, and we secured federal funding— two years, $250,000. And once more of the men were arrested, the community boarded up the pornography house and knocked it down.

But I don't want to overstate our success. In subsequent years, some of the men who had served their sentences began drifting back to Kalumburu; the statistic bandied about was that 13 per cent of the community's men were convicted sex offenders. A report from within the Department of Child Protection bemoaned a 'breakdown in social norms'. And less than 10 years later the region again made news when youth suicide rates reached 100 times the national suicide average.

In any event, in August 2008, I had to hand the program back to Judy and return to Canberra. My trial was starting in the Supreme Court.

***

My immediate worry was financial, as the barristers representing me asked for $55,000 upfront. By some miraculous coincidence, I got offered a couple of jobs for the Stolen Generation Alliance, facilitating major healing workshops that together earned me $35,000. And a rich friend loaned me the other $20,000. I stayed at Chris Graham's place—he and his wife ended up buying the rental property I had vacated after the police raid— because I had nowhere else to go in Canberra. My friends, as I've already mentioned, being somewhat thin on the ground, at that time.

On August 12, a week before the trial was scheduled to start, my legal team tried to stop the case proceeding, arguing that certain public service regulations prohibiting the disclosure of information—regulations the Crown insisted were relevant—were unconstitutional for various reasons. I won't bore you with the details, though that assumes I understand them all myself! The challenge failed anyway. Though if you Google my case you'll find it's the subject of legal debate, including if the law should be reformed so that Commonwealth officers who disclose classified information are not automatically liable to criminal sanctions.

Every morning at 7 o' clock in the week starting August 18, I headed to Ainslie Mountain in Canberra, a sacred place for us, the women's mountain for spiritual solace. And then I would go down to the Supreme Court where I sat all day, every day, contemplating a tableau that changed only slightly when witnesses came and went from the evidence box. Steadfastly in my corner: Arika, Chris Graham, my faithful, hardworking and emotionally invested lawyers, Jennifer Saunders and John Harris SC. Two Elders and their daughter, who I did not know, sat beside me in the gallery, returning every day, in a moving show of support.

Justice Richard Refshauge presided: he shocked me because with his strawberry blonde curls and boyish face he didn't look very judge-like.

I scanned the faces of the jurors—they were going to find me guilty, no doubt about it. Canberra was a public service town, after all. For a while I fixated on one, a no-nonsense-looking grey-haired woman in her forties. She was proper and exacting, you could tell. She'd find me guilty, for sure.

The hours dragged on as witness after witness swore an oath on the bible: the Mutitjulu youth workers, the IT experts in the public service who tracked my illicit email traffic. Greg wept. Dorothea was cagey and tight-lipped. No new information came to light, no dramatic revelations.

My mind returned to the judge. What was his life like outside the courtroom? Did he ski in winter, retreat to his coastal getaway in the summer? Mingle after-hours at some posh Commonwealth club? Was he married? Did his wife wear pearls and a twinset? Could my mind possibly tear itself free of clichés?

By the end of the week the jury was out for deliberations. Over the weekend, I pictured the proper lady in her 40s and steeled myself for the worst.

On Monday the jury returned. I was found guilty on five counts of leaking confidential material; the other two charges were dismissed. The jury was hung on whether I ratted out Rahm Adamedes to Dorothea after the meeting at Mutitjulu. My potential prison term had been whittled down from 14 years to a decade.

Reporting on the verdict, the *SMH* said about me: 'Outside court, she sang an Aboriginal song to rid herself of bad spirits'. I didn't!

At the sentencing on Monday, October 13, I was contrite before Justice Richard Refshauge—what else could I be? My actions were impulsive, but I was acting morally.

'I'm sorry,' I told him.

I came armed with great character references and reports; my psychiatrist, community activists, Judy Atkinson praised my work at Kalumburu. The judge rejected my narrative about conscientious leaking, and rebuked me. He said I had not disseminated the material for high-minded purposes but rather 'unacceptable motives'. I had not 'whole-heartedly' accepted the seriousness of what I had done. 'The conduct must be denounced, making light of it cannot be countenanced.'

The journos reckoned I was 'composed' as the judge read out his sentence. Fine of $2,000. Three-year good behaviour bond. No formal sentence was recorded. So, I *still* don't have a criminal record! After two years, untold hours, monumental stress and thousands of taxpayer dollars, this was the Government's return: $2000 and a rap over the knuckles. On the steps of the court, a media scrum waited. I regretted my actions, I told them, but I was trying to help the Mutitjulu community.

'I thought my role as a public servant was to actually support that community and the things they were trying to do. When you're a public servant in Indigenous affairs, sometimes you get to the point where you have to make a moral decision… People much higher than me in political life leak documents from cabinet level. Do they ever get charged and have to deal with two years of something like this?' I concluded by saying to the reporters, 'I did, I guess, one small thing to help my community… It's come to be shown that the Northern Territory intervention's been a huge imposition on us.'

On the latter point, do not take my word for it. Reams have been written about the intervention's harmful impacts on the communities it was supposedly engineered to save—a spike in the rates of suicide and self-harm, falls in school attendance, even more grog flowing in, even more violence making life miserable for women and children.

Needless to say, many others contest this bleak assessment, but it's not for me here to give a round-up on the stats and counter-stats. I know that during the intervention, my visits to Mutitjulu always left me feeling deflated and angry. There was a new police station—that much I'll give the authorities—and a turbo-charged law-and-order PR campaign. I once saw a vehicle paraded outside the station with a sign, 'This car was seized from a drug dealer'. But no serious new housing stock was built. And because the 'basics card' only worked in the supermarkets at Alice Springs, the less mobile Elders were left malnourished and starving, walking the streets in a daze.

And all of it, the whole plan, hinged on a pretext that was pure fiction. Not simply because of the 'fake youth worker'— about which the ABC remained unrepentant, an internal review concluding the descriptor was necessary to protect Andrews' identity—but also about what that digitised voice, and Minister Brough, had said. Neither the NT police nor the Australian Crime Commission, with its star-chamber powers, could substantiate claims of sex slaves or paedophile rings. 'No evidence whatsoever,' said the NT police about even the claim petrol was being exchanged for sex with children in Mutitjulu.

But wait, there's more. Greg's assertion that he had filed police statements about sex abuse in Mutitjulu and was forced to withdraw them because of threats to his family, was also shot down. The NT's chief Minister, Clare Martin, told parliament that during his time as a project officer in Mutitjulu, he never made a statement to police about paedophilia or violence in the community, although in May 2007, Lesley Calma *was* convicted of harassing him—'causing substantial annoyance', as the law framed it—and fined $600.

One ironic postscript to the 'fake youth worker' scandal: within five minutes of the *Lateline* segment's airing, Rahm Adamedes, the real youth worker at Mutitjulu, who by then had had his contract with the community terminated—officially because of funding issues, unofficially we know there was no love lost there—but was still living in the township behind what he described as 'a six-foot barbed wire fence', began receiving threatening phone calls accusing him of being the 'youth worker' on camera.

In truth, few people emerged from this murky and sinister affair untainted. About Greg, I have no taste for schadenfreude; he also suffered deeply—as anyone would if they were called 'disappointing' and untrustworthy—Clare Martin, again—under cover of parliamentary privilege. So great was his stress, he failed to front a Senate hearing in November that year. It was left to his boss, Wayne Gibbons, to insist that Greg had appeared on *Lateline* with the department's consent but not on its behalf.

Since the *Lateline* episode, Greg said he and his family were again subjected to constant threats and intimidation in the media and in the courtroom. They were forced to move house and accept police protection.

Then six years after my court case, Greg was appointed Australia's first 'Threatened Species Commissioner'.

I think we were all, in different ways, victims of a cynical and desperate government—and for all its macho call-in-the-military policy antics, the Howard Government still lost the 2007 election.

***

Leaving the Supreme Court that day in October, I counted my blessings and surveyed the wreckage—it could have been so much worse. Owing $90,000 in legal costs, I knew I had little choice but to declare myself bankrupt. Here I was, 50 and broke. So, when I told the judge and the media I regretted leaking, I meant it; in that moment the consequences of my actions—financial, professional, emotional—were bearing down on me.

In the years that followed, however, my sense of regret dissipated and my belief that I acted morally grew stronger. And after the trial, many people wanted a piece of me, even the renegade journalist, John Pilger—I appeared in his blistering documentary, *Utopia*.

Apparently, I was a whistleblower, a hero.

19

UNLOCKING THE DOOR

'**I** don't think I have much to tell you,' I told the lovely lady from the child abuse Royal Commission, 'cos I really just wanna give you some names'.

We had a good hour, hour and a half, available for the meeting, which had taken about nine months to schedule, for late 2013, in Canberra. But I really wasn't going to take long, I insisted, brisk, matter-of-fact. Arika stood at my side, eyes watchful. In the end we stayed more than two hours. I told the lovely commissioner everything. About the Aboriginal and Torres Strait Islander Catholic Council. About Longreach and Rockhampton. About the crimes against me and others.

I talked so much I almost forgot about handing over the names. So, the commissioner waited until I was done narrating, and prodded, gently.

'Would you like to give me the names? And would you like me to give them to the police? And even then, you don't have to do anything about it.'

'Oh, yes. That's my reason for coming. To give you the names.' The Royal Commission into Institutional Responses to Child Sexual Abuse came after a concerted campaign for a national inquiry into claims of systemic cover-ups in the Catholic Church over child sexual abuse. The terms of reference went beyond examining how the Catholic Church, or religious institutions in general, historically responded to allegations of child sexual abuse, encompassing schools, sports clubs and police. Since hearings had begun in April 2013, harrowing testimonies from victims about institutional indifference, or worse, of their trauma, dominated news bulletins and sparked renewed outrage.

And with these daily revelations, the relentless reporting, the last locked door in my mind was being prised open.

Earlier that year, at an information session for the Commission in Canberra, I learned that any member of the public could contact them with information, however vague. So, I wrote them a letter. I wanted to tell them about the paedophile priests who I would likely not get the chance to put in jail. They wrote back offering me a private meeting to discuss things further, which is how I ended up giving the commissioner names. Mick Hayes. Grove Johnson.

***

Some months after my meeting with the Commissioner, I admitted myself to hospital. I needed intensive therapy, and the only way to do that was to stay in my psychiatrist, Warwick's, clinic where they practised trauma and dissociation recovery, and where I could see him for three hours a week: to fill in the gaps and explore precisely what transpired when I was six, seven … eleven. The abuse had happened intermittently during primary school and then through high school, by different priests.

Mine is not a case of repressed memories—I always knew that what happened, happened. I carried around the fragmented images like litter. The presbytery at Longreach. My polka dot dress. The swinging fob watch. The mysterious white blisters and boils on my genitals, and the visits to 'Dr Tom' in an era when the term 'child sexual abuse' just wasn't part of our vocabulary.

During my early sessions with Warwick, I tentatively circled the perimeter. When I was a child, I told him, there was a group of priests who pushed the boundaries. They hung out with young people, drank with them. I heard later that some of them were abusing people I knew... Actually, I knew about the abuse even back then, at the time it was happening... In fact, one priest, Mick Hayes, abused some girls at Woorabinda mission and even got a 16-year-old pregnant; she named the child Michael, after his father.

But even once I overcame my wariness in therapy, I struggled to piece everything together; the details eluded me and I was happy to let them. As Warwick says, I had a dissociative response to trauma. For one thing, I was terribly young when the abuse started, and unlike the molestations of Leo Wright, Johnson's came without real preamble, without grooming—each time, a brutal *non sequitur*. And unlike Wright, Johnson never fessed up to his crimes.

I always intended to confront the whole truth—eventually; when I was ready for the kind of reckoning that makes us ill, pitting our bodies against ourselves.

***

'We've found out that this priest is still alive,' explained the policeman at the end of the line, roughly six months after my meeting with the Commissioner. He was talking about Grove Johnson. Mick Hayes, as I already knew, was dead.

'He's old. He lives in a place in Rockhampton. There are other victims of this priest.'

I can't recall if he waited for that news to sink in before continuing.

'But, you know, it costs a lot of money to put a priest in jail, do all the investigations. He's very old. As soon as we charge him, the Church is going to say he's got dementia.'

He didn't really think this was a case worth pursuing.

Silence.

'Well, can you tell me some stuff that happened?'

I was not feeling well when the phone rang. I was feeling even worse now. Not wanting to discuss Grove Johnson for one minute longer, I mumbled something and said goodbye. But not before he told me the names of two other victims, 'Mary' and 'Joseph'.

My old friend from Rockhampton, Colleen, rang to tell me 'Mary' was likewise a childhood friend of ours. We organised a catch-up with her. She sent me her police statement.

'I really want to charge him,' Mary told me. 'I gave the police my statement in 1996 and they've done nothing about it.'

Well, I said, now there were three of us. Even a public humiliation would be fine. This was July, shortly after my second three-week stint in hospital. In these weeks I drew a lot, talked a lot, remembered many things. Towards the end of my convalescence, Warwick said, 'You've got enough information to charge him if you want to'.

'I *really* want to do this,' Mary repeated.

I rang back the policeman. Explained that through a friend I'd been in touch with Mary, and we both wanted to make statements.

'Can you just tell me where the incidents happened and how old you were?'

This time, shakily, I could tell him. After a further attempt to talk me out of proceeding, the policeman referred me to a detective in Rockhampton.

In May 2015, my beloved Uncle Bob Randall died in Mutitjulu—his renown saw obituaries run in *The Economist* and

The Telegraph. I went up for the funeral, and afterwards travelled to Rockhampton, to the police station, where plainclothes Senior Constable Benjamin Podesta took my statement.

I understand the process is futile—the policeman was right, the authorities won't bother prosecuting an old man with no memory. But the Royal Commission has again demonstrated that for people in pain simply being heard can be tremendously healing.

As for public humiliation, Arika was right on to it. No sooner had I told her about Grove Johnson than she hunted for a photo of him on the internet and posted it on Facebook, telling the world, 'This man is a paedophile'. As an adult she is quite the advocate and very protective of me. She's especially angry with my mother for not being there for me when it mattered as a child. My mother often turned a blind eye to things my father did and if she knew something was going on, I don't think she knew exactly what it was. My father was definitely complicit in this but my daughter never really had the chance to get to know him as he died when she was a teenager and we had only visited Rockhampton a couple of times when she was a baby.

Poor Arika—she spent her primary school years with her father getting PTSD from being a war veteran, and her high school years with a mother who'd been recently diagnosed with DID (Dissociative Identity Disorder). No wonder she'd been eager for boarding school—anything to get away from her crazy mother and her sudden flights from shopping centres.

I didn't want to be crazy. I didn't want to be like William who wouldn't deal with his PTSD. At some point when Arika was in her teens, I felt she needed to know I was in therapy, so I said: 'Why don't you come and talk to Dr Middleton with me about all this so you can understand what I've got wrong with me?' After visiting him a few times where he explained what was wrong with me and what we were doing, she understood. And by the time she got to university she could see that I was on track to get well—just as I could see *she* was on track for a rewarding and meaningful future.

Like my parents, I've always believed that education is the key for a better future for Indigenous Australia; and seeing my daughter and her generation proudly taking on the world proves me right. These kids do not think of themselves as less worthy or less able than anyone else. They are proud of their Aboriginal heritage and want to keep the flame burning. In an interview with a Canberra University publication on her graduating from Arts—majoring in creative writing and journalism, for she's also her father's daughter—Arika said: 'My aim is to one day be a voice for my people, to teach others about who we are as a community and the oldest living culture on earth... I want to change the assumptions and judgements people automatically make about Aboriginal people rather than judging them on their actions as human beings.'

Despite years of turbulence, of shifting homes and simmering hostilities between me and William, despite her own battle with depression, my daughter blossomed into a wise, brave and compassionate young woman. She is my heartbeat.

In May 2018, four months before my memoir was released, Arika gave birth to her daughter Willa Grace, my first grandchild.

*****

In 1969, the contest for the regional swimming title was held at Rockhampton memorial pool. George and 11-year-old me travelled there, staying with a teammate's family. After the swimming meet, my father took me to the presbytery across the road from the cathedral. It was a sprawling mansion with a heavy, winding staircase at the centre. It must have been after lunch or tea time because there were people milling about in the ground-floor dining room, a low hum of conversation, the clinking of cutlery.

George fetched himself a cup of tea. Father Mick Hayes appeared—smiling, as always. Looking up at him strained my neck. George slipped away, leaving the two of us together. Father Hayes led me up the staircase. When we reached the second set of stairs, he yanked me close in the way he always did, with his famously strong grip.

We came to a long hallway, rooms branching off to the side. In one room, a tall ceiling, desk and chairs. A single bed.

'Do you know what we're here for?' he asked.

I knew well enough.

'Get on the bed.'

He told me to take off my clothes. I pulled down my underpants and pulled the sheet over me. He lay beside me, wriggled in the cramped space, wrapped his hands around my head.

'You know I only do this because I love you.'

The brushing sounds of his pants coming off. The air on my skin as he pulled the sheet from my body. Rubbing between my legs. As he climbed on top he was slobbering. I whimpered with pain, but he kept going till he was done. He rolled off from me. Got dressed.

'Wait,' he said. 'Your friend is here.'

Of course, he was. Father Grove Johnson reappeared every so often like a rodent. White shirt and black pants. Gold crosses on his lapels. His spectacles and ginger hair, his furtive manner. This time when he took out the fob watch, I said: 'You don't need to use that anymore'.

Father Johnson was even rougher. Afterwards, he left the room. I was dead like a piece of wood. Sore. I curled into a ball and sobbed. I used a shirt to wipe myself. Once I felt game to stand up, I peered out into the hallway for signs of life. About 10 minutes later, Father Hayes came back. It was time to go back downstairs, he said.

I waited in the front room for George to pick me up; when he came in, his face was inscrutable, as always. This began my deep anger towards my father for the rest of my life. He has since passed away; a heart attack took him three years after the Leo Wright case. And now my mother is in an aged care home, fading with dementia.

From the presbytery that afternoon, we returned to my team-mate's place, conveniently located near the swimming pool.

20

THE PERFECT DAWN

Since Uncle Bob moved back to Mutitjulu from coastal New South Wales in 2014, and still after his passing, I make several pilgrimages a year to Central Australia, visiting my adoptive Anangu family, learning more about the law, communing with our sacred places. In May 2017 I went again, shortly before the second anniversary of Bob's death, and in the vicinity of other important milestones: the 10-year anniversary of the Howard Government's NT intervention, the 50-year anniversary since the constitutional referendum when Australians voted to include Aboriginals in the census and allow the Commonwealth to make laws for them, and on the eve of an historic Indigenous summit on constitutional recognition.

Activists from around the country were descending on Uluru, mobilising and number-crunching, arranging logistics, yelling into their mobiles. They were determined to see the Convention give backing for a Treaty for Aboriginal Australia. We must resist the push for constitutional recognition, they argued—agree to that, and we undermine any real hope of self-determination for Indigenous peoples. In the townships at the foot of the rock, a restive, expectant energy hung in the dry air.

Maybe the pregnant moment had some bearing on why I startled awake one morning in the half-light, hearing the familiar call.

The previous day, a Sunday, I had arrived early at the aged care centre at Mutitjulu to take 'Nanna' Barbara Nipper AM, my teacher and a celebrated artist, for a day on homeland. I got there just as Nanna returned from the local Lutheran church— while no Christian, she does enjoy the singing. Her late husband, Nipper Winmati, Uncle Bob's grandfather, is the Elder brandishing the title deeds to Uluru in that iconic photograph in 1985 when the rock and surroundings lands were returned to their owners.

We packed a four-wheel-drive with blankets, paintbrushes, coloured twine, food supplies, damper, a small axe, a piece of wire for poking in the fire and branding, a curved wooden stump that bears a swirling black pattern, and a couple of frozen kangaroo tails from the supermarket. Leaving the township, we passed the house where the infamous meeting with the youth worker, Rahm Adamedes, was held 11 years earlier. I remembered one phone call with Uncle Bob about a year after the AFP raid, when I was working in Lismore, awaiting trial.

'We are never going to forget what you did for us.' He meant the price I paid in leaking information about the intervention to his family.

'You are a proper *Nungkari*.' I was a proper healer, a traditional medicine woman.

And that was the journey I embarked on as a young woman, ever since the four-day camp at the Hawkesbury River with the Aboriginal Elder Dance Theatre, when I first understood medicine was in my *tjukurpa*. Over the years I cultivated this calling, the soothing power of my ancestors guiding my hands, moving them over people's bodies, feeling within them currents of hot and cold, seeing colours. A university colleague with advanced breast cancer.

A troubled young boy from a very rich family in Marin County, California, who had stopped eating, his stomach distended as if he was a child of African famine—I rubbed yellow ochre on his belly and the next day he was eating again. In later years, I even took the Elders' advice about practising celibacy—just as I had earlier taken the same advice from Raja Yoga gurus—so that all my energy focuses on healing.

So, Uncle Bob said I had arrived as a *Nungkari*, that I was well on the road to Eldership. And that also happens to be the subject of my PhD, the task that consumed me for six years following my court trial—the impact of visionary and sacred leadership on community transformation, and the road to Eldership.

Now we were rumbling along the dirt roads to Umpiyara, Uncle Bob and Nanna Barbara's traditional homeland, about 15 minutes beyond Uluru. We set up at the bush camp and kindled a fire in the baking sun. Nanna Barbara sat crossed-legged in the red dust, skinning and roasting the kangaroo tail on the flame, branding the curved piece of wood, filing bark off a branch, weaving and singing. I helped fill in her dot paintings—one depicted a council of women deliberating around a campfire.

Nanna Barbara and Uncle Bob had dreamed of a thriving eco-tourism business centred around Umpiyara; precisely the sort of innovative economic development and visionary leadership the community was crying out for. They reckoned they could build a rammed-earth home out here, live out their old age close to the earth. But the venture faltered against red tape from government and the Land Council, and later, the NT intervention. Broken-hearted, Uncle Bob retreated to Mutitjulu where, thanks to the Federal Government's NT Emergency Response legislation in 2007, signs at the entrance decreed, 'No Pornography'.

Breaking the cycle of economic stagnation, social dysfunction and policy failure won't happen unless Aboriginals seize control of their own destiny, unless we put an end to the sham solutions of the past 30 years. I want to see a council of Indigenous Elders with equal status to the Australian Government, like the Sami have in Sweden—and most Indigenous people want it too.

A few weeks after my trip, following three days of deliberation, hundreds of Indigenous delegates at the summit adopted The Uluru Statement from the Heart, rejecting outright the prospect of mere recognition in the constitution, instead calling for a representative body to be enshrined in the nation's founding document and ultimately, a treaty. Five months later the Turnbull Government rejected the idea of a constitutionally-enshrined Indigenous 'Voice to Parliament', a stance that provoked instant outrage and hurt from Aboriginal leaders.

And so, my people's battle for dignity and power continues. When that thought gets me down, I remind myself of the words of a philosophical old blackfella I met many years ago. 'Look,' he said, winking, 'don't worry, *they* are only going to be here for a little while'. He clicked his fingers.

But all that—the gathering at Uluru, the statement and the response—was yet to happen on this morning when I roused in the half-light, hearing the call, feeling the magnetic pull. In the thick blue light, I threw on some clothes and grabbed the car keys. Passing the western side of Uluru, I averted my eyes. Too much male energy there, all those initiation ceremonies in the caves. In the past I've seen a man's face, sharp bones and thick lips, protruding from the sandstone surface. One sliver of rock strongly resembles a penis.

As I reached the eastern end, the women's site, all folds and crevices, the vast, clear sky was streaked pink. The lightest breeze in the air, like a whisper. I parked the car and jumped out, threw off my shoes, climbed through the low, flimsy fence. From the straggly yellow shrubs, I plucked a blade and placed it in my mouth, sucking gently.

I was cradled in the womb of our Earth Mother, in the place where all my Songlines converge. As the first rays of sun hit the rock-face her features sharpened into focus.

I spread my arms wide, raised them, palms facing the sky, and greeted the perfect dawn. Between my toes the red earth felt like silk.